THE ART OF HUNGARIAN PORCELAIN

PUBLISHED
FOR
THE 150TH ANNIVERSARY
OF THE
MANUFACTORY

GYŐZŐ SIKOTA

HEREND

THE ART
OF HUNGARIAN
PORCELAIN

PREFACE: DEZSŐ KERESZTURY

PÜSKI PUBLISHING, NEW YORK
CORVINA, BUDAPEST
1988

Title of the Hungarian original: Herend porcelánművészete
Műszaki Könyvkiadó, Budapest, 1973, 1981
Consultants: Tibor Szabó, Béla Felek and Imre Katona
Translated by Ervin Dessewffy
Photographs by József Németh
Design by Lajos Lengyel
Distribution throughout the world, with the
exception of the socialist countries

© Dr. Győző Sikota, 1973
Second edition
ISBN 963 13 2596 2
Printed in Hungary, 1988
Kossuth Printing House, Budapest
Published in co-production with Corvina Kiadó, Budapest
Additional copies may be ordered through Püski Publishing
251 E. 82nd Street, New York, N. Y. 10028
Telephone: (212) 879–8893 – (212) 734-3848
Library of Congress Cataloging in Publication Data
    Sikota Győző
        Herend
Library of Congress Catalog Card Number 87–062746
ISBN 0–915951–12–6

CONTENTS

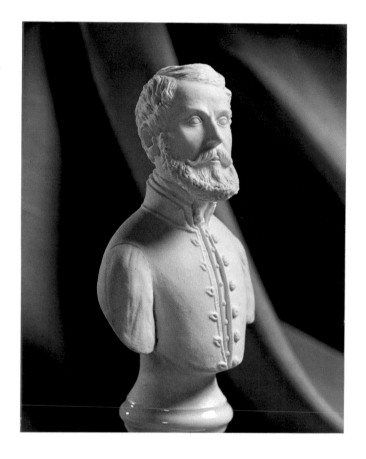

"Applied arts in Hungary once resembled a desolate plant blossoming in the Great Plain, spreading its scent unnoticed in shadowy silence. But now—or so I believe and pray to God that it may be true—it is about to bloom into a flower which the nation will take into its nurturing arms and shield against the gusty winds, so that it may become strong enough to stand up against all blows, from whichever direction they may come."[1]

Lajos Kossuth

PREFACE

It is always a pleasant, refreshing experience to walk the wide, modern halls of the Porcelain Factory of Herend, and not only because I have strolled many times through the somewhat patriarchal, old-fashioned rooms of the former manufactory at a time when my whole family was admiring the products of that workshop. Today, Herend continues to be the pride of the Hungarian ceramics industry; no doubt, the beauty of its products and the popularity of china throughout the world have much to do with it. Presently, Herend's fine quality porcelain is being exported to over forty countries.

In the spacious, sparkling clean halls, the newest machines perform the technical work, but the essence—the decorating and colouring of the porcelain—is done by hand. The men and women who work here are highly qualified designers contributing with their expertise and fine artistic sense to a superior team-work. Rightfully, Herend is recognized for being a cornerstone of industrial art, where good tradition is continued and supplemented with the best achievements of modern technology. Győző Sikota has compiled the results of his extensive, partly archival research into a monograph about the past and present of this Hungarian national institution. Since its publication in Hungarian, his book has become a fundamental work. Beautifully illustrated, it presents Herend and the art of making porcelain to the world.

Dezső Keresztury

FOUNDATION OF THE FACTORY

1826

A first glimpse of the Herend Porcelain Factory gives to visitors an immediate sense of its historic origins. The shallow curve of the arched entrance, with its friendly wooden door flanked by carved panels, is a vivid reminder of the nineteenth-century era of industrial expansion in Hungary. This was fostered under the fervent leadership of Lajos Kossuth, hero of the nationalist struggle, and sustained by the enthusiasm of the Hungarian people.[2] In 1976 we celebrated the one hundred and fiftieth anniversary of the Herend Porcelain Factory where porcelain was first manufactured in Hungary, and the skill of the craftsmen which ensured the success of the industry. For if the baroque entrance reminds us of the past, the modern buildings behind the courtyard indicate that here is an enterprise which has adopted modern techniques and is aware of future possibilities.

To achieve a clear understanding of the origins, traditions and development of the clay industry and the manufacture of porcelain in Hungary, we must go back to the feudal society of the fifteenth and sixteenth centuries. Documentary evidence dating from that period, found in libraries and in the archives of the craft guilds, also relics excavated on the sites of medieval settlements, provide clear proof that the art of ceramics has long been practised by the Hungarian people. New finds are constantly being made in the region of Veszprém which reveal the former existence of a highly-developed pottery industry. The isolation of the Hungarian villages resulted in a concentration of regional characteristics of both form and motif powerfully fostered by local taste. All non-indigenous forms and motifs were modified so that a local tradition developed in which national and local features were combined. One example of this fusion is the adoption throughout Hungary of a superior method of using tin for glazing, an innovation directly resulting from the lead-glazing used by local potters.

Parallel with the emergence of local folk pottery, towards the end of the fifteenth century, King Matthias Corvinus inaugurated a majolica factory which assumed the lead in the production of majolica throughout Europe with the single exception of Italy where it originated.[3] In Florence and in Hungary a flourishing industry began

9

to produce floor coverings, splendid serving dishes and stove tiles with relief ornamentation incorporating the emblems of King Matthias and Queen Beatrice. These promising developments were halted by the Turkish invasion which heralded a period of subjection lasting one hundred and fifty years.

It was therefore only at the beginning of the seventeenth century that Hungarian craftsmen began once again to produce pottery of artistic merit. The majolica produced in factories and the pottery produced by members of the guilds was enriched partly by characteristically Turkish forms and motifs, partly by the colourful style of the South German faience introduced by the Habans, who, at the end of the sixteenth century, were driven out of Switzerland because of their Anabaptist faith, and settled in our country.

Most of the Haban-influenced earthenware is decorated with yellow, blue, green and manganese violet tendrils on a white background. In form and motif these products conformed to the popular demand for the Renaissance style already to be found in Central Europe. They were however made by superior techniques and were of greater artistic merit, qualities which strongly influenced the development of Hungarian pottery. At the same time, the relics originating from the Habans clearly show a gradual adoption of the Hungarian styles. Haban pottery was definitely influenced by a new environment. Soon after its introduction popular motifs of Hungarian folk-art were incorporated in the decoration—the tulip, the carnation and the pomegranate. Later, during the reign of Maria Theresa, harassed by Church and State, the Habans were converted to Catholicism and gradually integrated with the peoples of Upper Hungary and Transylvania. Their descendants still tended to cultivate the traditions of their forebears, but by the middle of the nineteenth century the Haban style was no longer being applied in Hungarian potteries which, as elsewhere in Europe, were adapting to a change in taste.[4]

It is interesting to learn—from research undertaken by Imre Katona—that Haban art continued to exert some influence in the county of Veszprém, certain regions of Transdanubia and the county of Vas. The Öskü Guild Jug is a relic from this area. We can also trace potters of Anabaptist origin who, in the second part of the eighteenth century, migrated from Upper Hungary to Transdanubia.

Lead-glazed guild jugs dating from the eighteenth century, with engraved and relief decoration, originating from the region of Veszprém bear witness to local affection for pottery wares as well as skill in making them. These jugs are now treasured in our museums as precious examples of the folk pottery from which we can appreciate the respect of the people of Veszprém for their own arts and crafts. Towards the end of the eighteenth century Hungarian potters had to face serious competition from makers of faience who, to evade the industrial tariffs imposed by Austria, established themselves in a number of European centres and finally in Hungary.

The first of these majolica factories was founded in 1743 by Francis of Lotharingia, later the Holy Roman Emperor Francis I and the husband of Maria Theresa.[5] With a variety of late-baroque products the factory soon attained a prestigeous position within the world of ceramics. Tableware and figurines, elaborate and richly coloured to please the Emperor, had also the personal touch favoured by the Queen. A seemingly endless series was produced of small sculptures depicting scenes and themes from the Bible, mythology, and the natural world of plants and animals. These are now for the most part in museums or private collections. With the enthronement of Joseph II, the baroque-rococo era came to a sudden end. The new king ordered a switch to the manufacture of "hard" pottery, stronger but not so attractive. This marked the beginning of the factory's gradual decline. It fell to János György Eger, oil manufacturer, as the Pest-Buda commissioner of the factory at Holics, to undertake a very difficult sale of Holics products at the famous Kemnitzer House on the bank of the Danube. It was in 1827 that faience ceased to be produced at Holics.

Factories were now producing not faience but stoneware for which there was more demand. By the end of the eighteenth century, stoneware factories had been established all over Europe. This temporarily satisfied the needs of the middle classes for whom the price of porcelain was too high.

Influenced by this trend new factories were established, a very costly undertaking, at the beginning of the nineteenth century, in the county of Veszprém. This marks the beginning of a significant chapter in the history of Hungarian ceramics. It was a heroic era of technical progress and artistic achievement when the foundations were laid for our present ceramics and porcelain industry in Hungary, an era which has been the subject of many scholarly studies.

In his "History of the Pottery Factory of Pápa", Bertalan Kéry refers to the close contact established between the various factories built in the late eighteenth and early nineteenth centuries. "Labourers and foremen wandered from one factory to another. In the first half of the nineteenth century, the County of Veszprém established itself as the Transdanubian centre for ceramics: Pápa, Városlőd, Herend and Bakonybél were manufacturing either hard pottery or porcelain. These centres were united geographically, as well as by their collective use of raw materials available on land owned by the Veszprém diocese. Labour was provided by common workforce. In the area as a whole there remained local features in the products though many features were common to all factories."

Such an established tradition of ceramic art might well have served as a basis for the foundation of Herend. In the sixteenth and seventeenth centuries the European ceramics industry was greatly influenced by a new awareness of Chinese porcelain, increasingly imported at that time. The superior quality of Chinese porcelain and the wide range of magnificent colours used to decorate it inspired among European craftsmen a search for the secret of the Chinese manufacturing process. It was an occupation that promised its own reward, for Chinese porcelain was so expensive that it could be seen only on the tables of the wealthiest of the ruling princes.[6]

Organized experiments were doomed to failure. The secret of porcelain remained a secret but the experiments were helpful in that they indicated a way to make white earthenware. It was in fact by chance that the secret of porcelain manufacture finally reached Europe.

An alchemist by the name of Böttger, in the service of King William of Prussia, was attempting to produce gold. Böttger, seemingly doubtful of his capability in this task, escaped to Saxony, where the Saxonian Prince had him locked up in the castle of Koenigstein, so that Böttger might produce gold for him. The Prince provided him with everything necessary for his experiments, including raw materials. Böttger worked diligently in his laboratory until one day, while trying to extract liquid gold out of a certain type of fired clay, he found a new material with a smooth shell-like surface which did not absorb water. This material resembled porcelain and though it was more brown than white, Böttger realized that he was on the way to making porcelain. Success came when he found himself in possession of kaolin. It was then that the Elector of Saxony, Augustus the Strong, founded the first European porcelain factory.[7]

The beautiful porcelain which was now produced in the factory at Meissen—statuettes, richly embellished or decorated with miniature paintings—marked the beginning of the race to secure the secret still closely guarded in the factory on the shore of the River Elbe.[8]

The monopoly so long held by the Chinese and the Saxons was soon broken. Royal porcelain factories were established in Vienna, Sèvres, Berlin, St. Petersburg (now the Lomonosov Factory, Leningrad), and Copenhagen.[9] Parallel with these developments the production of faience and stoneware at Holics was emulated elsewhere, factories being established around the turn of the nineteenth century at, for example, Pápa, Kassa (now Košice in Czechoslovakia), Batiz (now Rumania), Igló (now Novares, Czechoslovakia), Városlőd, Apátfalva and Hollóháza.

In Hungary the initiation of the porcelain industry took place rather later than elsewhere in Europe, for the most part in the early years of the nineteenth century when the industrialization of the country had scarcely begun.[10] Trades traditionally organized by the guilds were faltering under the pressures of foreign competition and especially the oppressive tariffs imposed by Austria. Craftsmen were hampered by lack of transport, even more by the lack of schools in which apprentices might learn their chosen trades.

The Reform Period (1825—1848) with its plans for industrialization inspired the Hungarians with hope. The development of the porcelain industry became almost synonymous with the idea of reform. Thus, Herend porcelain is virtually the child of the Reform Period. Nevertheless, the porcelain factory of Vienna, founded soon after the secrets of Meissen were revealed, continued to dominate the Hungarian market and thwarted the development of the industry in Hungary. Yet before the close of the eighteenth century the processes in the manufacture of porcelain had been publicized widely, even in print. Artisans who worked in the porcelain factories had the restlessness in their veins. They moved from factory to factory and from country to country acquiring new skills and sharing their own knowledge of the art and technology of porcelain making in Hungary.

The rise of the Hungarian porcelain industry is linked with the names of Count István Széchenyi and Lajos Kossuth, both prominent figures of the Reform Period, a movement which advocated political independence for Hungary, the abolition of feudal privileges and support for the middle classes. While travelling in England, Széchenyi came to the conclusion that the Hungarian aristocracy must make their own contribution to the industrialization of their country. He persuaded his friend, Ferdinand Berczenheim, to offer the kaolin discovered on his estates[11] to his own countrymen so that they could establish a porcelain factory in Hungary. Prompted by Széchenyi, Berczenheim looked beyond his own interest in profit and lucrative investment and sought to further the national interest. He realized that it had been given to him to initiate the manufacture of porcelain in Hungary. Thus, the first Hungarian porcelain factory was established and production started in 1827. When smoke first rose from the chimneys of Telkibánya, Széchenyi's hopes had been realized and Telkibánya became a milestone along the road to industrialization in Hungary.

This national success was followed by an achievement of European impact, the foundation of a second porcelain factory, in the remote village of the Bakony mountains, Herend. This too was a product of the Reform Period: the Telkibánya factory owed its existence to Széchenyi, while Herend developed under the patronage of Kossuth. A well-known difference of opinion between Széchenyi and Kossuth was reflected in the further development of the two factories, and this explains why Kossuth extended his support only to Herend.[12]

Recently, the history of the porcelain factory at Herend has become a favourite subject for research. New facts have emerged, especially in 1966, when a conference was organized by the Hungarian Academy of Sciences, the Veszprém County Museum and the Herend Porcelain Factory. The date when the factory was founded has been a subject of some controversy, though in many publications it has always been given as 1839, while the name of the founder has been given as Mór Fischer. Now, however, documents have been discovered which reveal that before 1839, on the estates of the Bishop of Veszprém, there was a pottery workshop where experiments were made in an attempt to produce porcelain.[13] These efforts are attributed to Vince (Vinzenz) Stingl of Sopron who, according to the documents, owned both the land and the pottery until June 3, 1840. In 1842 *Pesti Hírlap* recorded that "as far back as fourteen years ago, the raw material for making porcelain was found in Herend, within the County of Veszprém, where experiments were conducted in an attempt to produce porcelain, but over a period of eleven years the products were yellow, grey and imperfect." According to this report it would seem that the factory at Herend already existed around 1828. These facts, however, were submerged in the publicity, ably fostered by Mór Fischer, which surrounded Herend during the 1840s. Thus Fischer eventually came to be regarded as the founder, and the name of Stingl was forgotten. Dating from the forties, there are innumerable press references, local and foreign, to the "Herend Porcelain Factory, Mór Fischer, 1839". By contrast there is a comment in the July 11, 1922 issue of *Szózat* as follows: "In Herend they know otherwise," a comment which provoked a lawsuit initiated by Fischer's grandson Jenő Farkasházy, who had a vested interest in the claim that Fischer was the founder, and it was his hope that the name of Stingl would pass into oblivion.

Vince Stingl was born in Sopron, in 1814, of plebeian ancestry. He began to earn a living in the city of Pápa by illustrating playing cards, but five years later he had become technical director of the stoneware factory owned by the widow of György Schlögl in the city of Tata. He had to leave Tata after Moses Aron Fischer, cousin of the Herend Fischer, accused him of a lack of basic knowledge which resulted in "terrible losses".

Subsequent records show that he was in Herend in 1825. According to the Veszprém County Records, on November 1, 1825, Vince Stingl borrowed 1,730 forints from Domokos Stöckl, parish priest of Kislőd, repayable at six per cent.[14] Since the inflation following the Napoleonic wars had by then abated, Stingl received the 1,730 forints in new money. This relatively large sum indicates that Stingl left Tata with a minimal amount of capital, but also that his intention was to invest in a small factory, and not in a retail pottery. This is substantiated by his subsequent borrowings. A number of small potteries active in Hungary during the nineteenth century had been founded by members of the aristocracy, or under the auspices of the Church. It was a good way of making money that was soon followed by ambitious members of the middle classes. Lack of capital often necessitated borrowing, sometimes to pay for a lease on the property, or to expand the business. The source of these loans was usually a noble patron, a wealthy merchant or, as in the case of Herend, dignitaries of the Church. The earliest authentic evidence associating Vince Stingl with the foundation of a ceramics factory dates from 1826. The minutes of Veszprém County Assembly, October 10th, 1826 record that: "The noble free and royal city of Sopron officially announces that Vince Stingl, potter of Herend, is obliged to pay to his brother, János Stingl soldier of the Hessen-Hamburg regiment" 79 forints 10 7/10 fillérs as his share of an inheritance.[15]

Further proof is provided by the minutes of the County Assembly later that same year: "Vincentius Stingle Figulus vel amphorarius Geschirrmacher in posessione Herend"—works in Herend in the craft of ceramics.[16]

In those days it was not unusual to find potters described in a variety of different ways—sometimes fabricators, sometimes stoneware manufacturers. In the Roman Catholic birth-registers, the workers in stoneware factories, at Hollóháza for instance, are listed as "porcelain workers". Furthermore, regardless of what they actually produced, the establishments themselves were sometimes called stoneware factories, sometimes porcelain factories. Such inconsistencies occur very often in the references to Stingl.

Why did he choose this insignificant, as yet unknown and sparsely-populated region of Bakony, instead of one of the well-known sites of the long-established potteries, such as Pápa or Városlőd, where the necessary raw materials were much more readily available? Records dated 1827 reveal that he even had to procure timber, clay and sand from land owned by József Kopácsy, Bishop of Veszprém around Lőd, and from Csehbánya, Alsóerdő and Kislőd. To the cost of materials he had to add the cost of transport. On the other hand, by selecting the Miklós Mansion for his factory site (the Miklós family were mill owners) he secured a mill which could easily be converted to grind the paste. Although Stingl had been determined to build his factory in the Lőd region, it appears that he could make a more favourable agreement with the Miklós family than with the bishop, for the Miklós family were from Pápa and already known to him. Indeed his association with Pápa was by no means insignificant: it was the Schlögl family connection that had enabled him to gain a position in the stoneware factory at Tata and his own family resided in Pápa during the first decades of the nineteenth century. However, he could not quite free himself from the authority of the Church even when he had moved far from Kislőd.

From 1834 onwards there were several court actions between the insolvent Stingl and the Bishop. "Vincze Stingl, porcelain maker at Herend has in the year 1827 become indebted to His Excellency, in the amount of 1087 forint and 24 fillérs, for various, mostly occupation-related goods".

Documents relating to Stingl's activities at Herend between 1826 and 1839 refer to gloomy days of struggle. There was a shortage of capital, a need to borrow, and anxiety about purchases and transport of material. It was a heavy responsibility to obtain qualified staff, for the initial success of the enterprise depended on trained and skilful painters, inventive model makers and conscientious kiln operators. In spite of the regular influx of itinerant potters it was very difficult to find well-trained employees for a newly-established factory.

There is no documentary evidence relating to Stingl's workforce and their working conditions. We have to rely on contemporary archives such as the local registers of births, marriages and deaths in which it is possible to discover some of the names of workers at the Herend factory. For example the parish register of Szentgál dated October 15, 1837 records the name of József Tántzka, "porcelain-apprentice aged 35 years and János Rettig aged 30 years"; also that of Ferenc Vintsigel (Windschügel), who was constantly in financial difficulties and who took up permanent residence in Herend.[17]

Some additional information has come to light concerning Stingl's first factory. Whereas it seemed that the venture was developed by only two men, Vince Stingl and his partner János Mayer (who joined Stingl only in 1839, for which reason we have attributed to Stingl all achievements between the years 1825 and 1839), there is a reference to three workers in the Herend factory in the 1828 register, Stingl being one of them. However, Gábor Pap, the author of the 1837 newspaper article and a contemporary, makes no mention of Stingl's two colleagues, and from the wording of his article we may well conclude that even in 1837, Stingl was conducting his experiments alone, without assistance. Yet, judging by the length of these experiments, this would seem to have been virtually impossible, especially when one considers how much more complex is the process for the manufacture of porcelain compared to that of stoneware. In Vienna—where he studied—the stages of manufacture were highly specialized. The workers specialized in either grinding, paste-mixing or firing, while yet others were responsible for the decoration. Thus we have concluded that the "opifex" (handicraftsman) who was listed—unfortunately anonymously—in the 1828 register was Stingl's paste-maker.

We know from other sources that in 1839 the Herend factory increased the range of its activities so that around the mid-thirties: "...its name began to be known, when finally, and after a long period of struggle it started to produce acceptable porcelain... It was Vince Stingl (registered in 1828 as Stengl) ... who inaugurated the manufacture of porcelain ... on the present site of the factory; he joined forces with a modeller called Paffmann or some similar name, then with a potter by the name of Pullmann from the region of Szepesség." This brief note confirms that Pullmann was a later colleague and that Stingl conducted his experiments together with Paffmann. Thus it is clear that the "opifex" listed in the 1828 register was indeed Paffmann, whom Stingl had probably known from the time when he first arrived in Herend.

Pullmann presumably joined him later, for Stingl was initially experimenting in the production of "tin-glazed white-pottery." Pullmann may well have been responsible for the daily operation of the factory during these experiments. (Incidentally, the name Pullmann is of Haban origin. In the eighteenth and nineteenth centuries a number of families known by this name were living in Hungary, especially in Upper Hungary.)

Vince Stingl founded the factory of Herend at a time when the ceramics industry throughout Europe was changing radically to meet a soaring demand for ceramics and porcelain. The middle-classes had survived the temporary crisis following the Napoleonic wars, and now their purchasing power reflected their growing prosperity. In the early nineteenth century, especially in Western Europe, public taste responded to the increased production of porcelain which now became very fashionable. The stoneware factories were trying to compete with the demand for porcelain by improving the quality and design of their products. Most factories produced both stoneware and porcelain. In Pápa, in the county of Veszprém, the stoneware factories began to produce porcelain, and with considerable success. Stingl was ready to move with the tide. He allowed neither his experiments nor his lack of capital to stand in the way. He borrowed more and more money and devoted all his energy to improving the quality of his products, making use of technical innovations, supervising the administration of the factory and promoting sales. But in spite of all his hard work, he could not meet the demands of his creditors to whom he now had to bind himself to repay his debts:

"Proceedings for the recovery of debt, City of Világos, between the Right Reverend János Küllei, Canon and Provost of Veszprém as Plaintiff, and Vincze Stingl, porcelain-maker and lessee of the Herend Porcelain Factory as Debtor and Defendent. Charta Bianca. Of One Hundred (100) V forints which I received from the Right Reverend János Küllei, Canon of Veszprém, in order to effect the necessary additions to my porcelain factory in Herend, for the purchase of all necessary material and equipment, I now agree to pay interest due, also to repay the full amount on the next New Year's Day. I offer to the above Gentleman, as collateral security, the factory founded by me, with all its contents and products as well as all my other assets. Signed, Veszprém, Aug. 16, 1827."[18]

Harassed by the needs of a growing family, pressed by other creditors and worried by problems within the factory, Stingl was unable to repay his debt to the Canon. The Church again had recourse to the law and at a meeting held in Stingl's house in Herend, in the presence of two witnesses, János Drexter and Ádám Eizenhoffer, the legal representative of the episcopal estates announced the decision of the Chief Justice to impose a so-called "execution sum" which amounted to 261 forints.

We know from records that between the years 1825 and 1830, Stingl borrowed some three and a half thousand forints.[19] It is well documented that he used these funds for the development of his factory, but to no avail, as the amounts were too small for him to keep pace with the rapid development of the ceramics industry. In 1846, Domokos Zichy, Bishop of Veszprém, spent 12,000 forints to modernize the equipment of the factory in Városlőd, so that porcelain could be made there.[20] Stingl's small pottery had started with the production of stoneware befitting the taste and styles of the time. One relic of this period is a plate (c. 1828), made of hard clay, ornamented with embossed cobalt lines and bearing a unique Herend mark, which is now in the Museum of Applied Arts.[21] János Mayer's memory is kept alive by a stoneware soup plate formed in the style of the Vienna factory, with a "Mayer J. Herend" mark (1839), and this too can be seen in the Museum of Applied Arts.

One cannot but wonder whether around that time porcelain had already been produced at Herend. However, the production of both stoneware and porcelain has been well documented. Thus the written evidence seems to suggest that Vince Stingl attempted to make porcelain in Herend before the arrival of Fischer. It is quite probable that with more capital Stingl might have achieved a greater success both artistically and commercially. Harassed by creditors and the threat of lawsuits, financial anxieties finally drove him to negotiate with his former rival, who had sufficient capital to save the factory.

With the appearance of Fischer in 1839, a short but nevertheless creative period of the factory's history came to an end.

Stingl may evoke pity but he also commands our admiration. He was only one of many Hungarians who failed as manufacturers of porcelain because of lack of capital combined with stiff competition. As a result of our scientific research we feel a sense of obligation to pay tribute to Stingl with: "Herend 1826, Stingl!" This tribute in no way reflects on the achievements of Fischer who lived to see the fruits of his labour, and is rightly honoured for his contribution to porcelain manufacture in Hungary, but it is beyond doubt that it was Stingl who initiated the earliest production of porcelain at Herend.

In the archives of 1837 to 1840, references to Fischer attribute to him a role somewhat similar to that of a banker, a man who lent money and bought property to secure the highest possible return on his capital. He provided the capital used by Stingl and János Mayer to buy the lease of the Herend site.[22] It is doubtful whether this arrangement constituted a legal agreement. It is possible that Fischer was able to manipulate the settlement without recourse to any binding agreement, a procedure he had already used in both Tata and Pápa. His early confrontation with Stingl and the fact that the loan was given before Stingl and Mayer bought the lease would seem to indicate the lack of a legal agreement. As a bankrupt, Stingl had no alternative but to negotiate with Fischer whose money he needed to save the factory.

As recorded in the protocol of the County Council meetings, Stingl borrowed a total of 3,170 forints between October 6, 1839 and the end of 1840; during the same period János Mayer borrowed another 1,800 forints. Most probably Fischer later deducted these loans when he bought the factory. The fact that Mayer also received loans indicates that he was in legal partnership with Stingl. Fischer thus obtained the factory as a result of a premeditated plan, just as he later schemed to drive out Stingl who at the time was still employed in the factory. Ousted from Herend, Stingl moved to Városlőd where "in January 1847 he worked in the stoneware factory of Count Domokos Zichy, Bishop of Veszprém, as overseer."[23] After the summer of 1847 there are no more records of him either in Városlőd or anywhere else in the Hungarian ceramics industry.

ROAD TO SUCCESS

1839–1846

With the advent of Fischer a new era began at Herend, for he had enough capital to concentrate on the production of fine quality goods.[24] According to his own handwritten balance sheet, he provided some forty thousand forints of working capital in 1840. He no longer risked his own cash on other ventures but invested only in the factory of Herend, his sole ambition being to compete successfully with the highest quality porcelain produced elsewhere in Europe and to extend his markets to increase his profits. The archives of Veszprém contain legal documents dating from the 1840s indicating that Fischer had recourse to court action concerning the fulfilment of contracts undertaken by masons, carpenters and engineers. Thus we learn of the installation of five enamel-mills and four grinding machines during the early forties. The newspaper *Pesti Hírlap* confirms the rate of expansion in a report that the factory had obtained a Meissen-type, three-compartment Haban kiln, and was "in the process of buying two more". Technical innovation constituted the major problem. Next came the difficulty of securing well-trained workers. It was during this period that new laws were being drawn up by the Reform-Parliament. In an attempt to employ all available resources for the benefit of the country, laws were introduced which had the effect of undermining the guild system, and permitted industry to "employ any and all help, unskilled labourers without restrictions". So the local potters became wheel-operators, and a good number of foreign porcelain-workers, mostly painters, gained employment. The *Pesti Hírlap* appealed to the people of Veszprém county to buy Herend porcelain, pointing out that "most of the workers are local, they are offered employment all the year round … and have the opportunity to have their sons trained in one of the most notable of our industries".[25] By 1841 fifty-four people were employed, suggesting production on a substantial scale. From October 1840 to November 1841 the merchandise produced from one kiln alone was worth 15,962 forints and 21 fillérs, while the cost of modernization during the years 1839–40 amounted to 26,785 forints and 57 fillérs.

Fischer now began to consider enlarging the factory buildings, and in 1840 he purchased a property previously rented from Chief Constable Pál Barcza.

Fischer's ambitions went beyond the bounds of what was feasible at the time. He hoped to achieve total modernization of the manufacturing process, using only the most advanced technology. In the period when Stingl owed him so much money that he himself practically owned the factory, he gave no thought to the problem of managing it without the assistance of the man who had launched the enterprise and who had sustained it because of his own technical knowledge and expertise. Stingl left Herend, taking with him his accumulated knowledge, the results and secrets of his eleven-year-long experiments, unappreciated by Fischer who had manœuvred to get him out of the way. Fischer was left in possession of the factory but without a knowledge of the secrets of porcelain manufacture. For there were still secrets. It was a subject for research in the universities of Austria, Germany, Czechoslovakia and Poland; textbooks were published by Baumgarten and Littrow and translated into Hungarian. Nevertheless, there were processes that could be learnt only through long years of familiarity with expensive and obscure raw materials and by continuous experiment. Kaolin may have been known as an essential component of the paste but it was a fine art to mix it with clay, quartz and feldspar in the right proportions. The correlation of the paste and the glaze is equally important to avoid hairline cracks. A knowledge of innumerable types of glaze and paste is essential. Such knowledge is acquired only after long years of experience. Stingl's experience was lost to Herend and Fischer had to survive without him. Mayer alone remained to give continuity to the production, while Fischer—learning from Stingl's eleven-year-long experiments—tried to operate the expensive factory on which he had expended so much time and money. Thus, unaware of essential processes, without even knowing where to obtain the kaolin used at Herend, he could not risk the economic and moral consequences of another ten years of experiment. We know that Fischer conducted experiments lasting several years and the diary in which he recorded the firings are in the archives of the Museum of Applied Arts. His notes tell us what type of merchandise was produced in Herend between 1841 and 1844, also his reasons for using a variety of components for his pastes. Two of the firing dates were January 3, 1842, and February 1, 1842, and the diary was kept from 1841 to 1843; it is clear that these were years of intense activity for Fischer. There are also entries of gravel deliveries with no indication of the calendar year, the first May 20, the last, in a different handwriting, January 4. All entries, except the last, refer to successive dates. It seems that kaolin was brought from Zettlitz. Other raw materials such as quartz came from a variety of places, and were often referred to by local names. The gravel had originally come from Sopron, then in January 1841, gravel arrived from Abelsbierg. The high cost of the Zettlitz kaolin must have prompted the change. For a trial firing on March 18, 1842, Zettlitz kaolin was mixed with large quantities of rhyolith from Passau and Regensburg, but sand from Városlőd was added as a precaution against failure. It seems that the experiment did not succeed, for by the end of the same month (August) we find a note concerning another experiment with pastes and glazes in which pure Zettlitz kaolin was used. At Herend the Városlőd-kaolin or rhyolith-kaolin was used together with Városlőd-gravel in the manufacture of porcelain. It would seem that in all these experiments Fischer was primarily anxious to find a substitute for the expensive and rare Zettlitz-kaolin. But he was also concerned to improve the quality of his paste. However, it is only in diary entries for November 1841 (13, 15, 18, 23) that Fischer noted his satisfaction with the paste used. *("Diese Massen waren die schönsten.")* Obviously these were the formulas used for making the basic paste from then on. This accounts for the fact that there is a variation in the composition of the paste—either as to the nature of the constituents or the proportions in which they were used. The method most often used to improve the paste was to grind some already fired earthenware or porcelain particles into the mixture. Probably leftover, experimental porcelain objects from the Stingl era were used. This would explain why there is no Herend porcelain from the period before 1840 in our museums. The products dating from 1840 begin to reveal the effects of improved technique and the employment of more highly-trained craftsmen.

Under Fischer's management the factory at first produced porcelain to suit the contemporary taste for neo-baroque. It was also marked by the influence of Czech

I

2

porcelain. Fischer did not aspire to the creation of a new artistic style, for he did not think of himself as either an artist or a craftsman. At first, therefore, he manufactured only easily marketable useful objects. The Viennese, empire-style porcelain with under-glaze cobalt blue "Rantfl Muster" decoration is typical of this period.

There is no such simplicity of form and decoration in the Herend porcelain produced in the following year when Fischer, endeavouring to compete with the Viennese and Czech manufacturers, began to produce goods of higher quality. He was secure in the knowledge that the early, simple shapes with line or flower decoration were in demand, inexpensive, and producing an annual revenue of 5,000 forints. For some time the factory was also turning out high quality fire-resistant bricks, previously imported from Vienna. Fischer, encouraged by his early financial success, began to extend the range of his products. He also wanted to publicize the factory beyond the mountains of Bakony, and he applied for "appointment to the Crown" in 1841, where upon his establishment was granted the title of "Imperial and Royal Char-

22

tered Porcelain Factory", while the right to include the Imperial Royal Eagle in its signs and marks was granted by the Council of the Board of the Governor General. On February 7, 1842, the General Assembly of the county of Veszprém, using the enthusiastic language of the Reform Period, issued their award: "By Order of the County this privilege is granted together with the right to use the Imperial and Royal Eagle coat of arms on the understanding that embedded in it will be the coat of arms of Hungary. As an expression of patriotism ... in the future it will be displayed only under the coat of arms of Hungary."[26]

After the initial uncertainty of his first years, Fischer began to study the technical and artistic achievements of his Viennese competitors. The porcelain dating from the 1840s demonstrates the competitive quality of the Herend factory. Very soon Herend porcelain had become comparable, in form and decoration, with that made in Vienna. Thus, when Herend porcelain was displayed at the first Hungarian industrial exhibition in 1842, it was greeted with surprise and delight. In his official report, Lajos Kossuth acclaimed it as capable of "satisfying the demands of any princely table". And his reference to Vienna was quite deliberate: "We do not say that Hungarian porcelain can, at this moment, compete with that of Vienna, but we do say that no one, looking at the porcelain set on the table of the Prince Primate would think that our local product could not add to the beauty of even the most ornate table."[27] One may well wonder that after such praise Fischer had to be satisfied with a bronze medal, when a certain Dénes Szerecsen, who exhibited only a small piece of black Chinese ink for Rosenau, was awarded the gold medal. The factory was fully compensated for this neglect by the support of people who, by now familiar with the products, began to buy more and more Herend porcelain. The most valuable support still came from Kossuth who continued to publicize the factory and provide financial assistance.

One of the exhibits was a translucent biscuit panel portraying Bishop József Kopácsy who, as Bishop of Veszprém, had been known to Stingl. It is now in the Museum of Applied Arts. The mark on the panel is: "Móric Fischer at Herend 42 S". Later Fischer used only his initials MF. The number 42 indicates the date of manufacture. The favourable reception of the Herend exhibits at the first Hungarian Industrial Exhibition established the factory's reputation. Fischer felt empowered to invest more capital, organize the regular use of a Meissen-type kiln, buy new property from Pál Barcza, extend existing buildings and so increase production. His aim was to achieve a 50,000 forints per year turnover and to turn raw material costing 6 forints into products worth 100 forints.[28]

On March 18, 1843, his dreams were shattered when fire broke out in the factory, causing incalculable damage. The General Assembly of the County of Veszprém feared that this national bastion of the porcelain industry was facing annihilation.[29] Dénes Molnár, Chief Constable of the county reported that "Móric Fischer's Herend factory, built at enormous cost, an enterprise which gave a livelihood to many tax-paying citizens ... a factory associated with the founding of our national industry

... has been destroyed, also the workers' cottages and the store rooms, by a criminal incendiarist ... causing damage estimated at 12,000 forints."[30]

The factory in flames is depicted on a beautifully painted porcelain plate, probably made at a later date. The 848-pastemark might be the date of the fire.

Fischer survived this crisis with characteristic determination and open-handedness. He turned to the Hungarian people who were anxious to see the development of Hungarian industry, and with the help of his personal connections he obtained loans. A willing staff and his own administrative ability brought him through the next difficult years. Production continued even while the repairs were still in progress, and the factory managed to participate in the national exhibition of 1843.

The First National Exhibition had greatly stimulated the nation's economy. Encouraged by this first success and anxious to extend it, the leaders of industry organized the Second National Exhibition with many more participants. Kossuth himself presented the awards, based on decision by jury, including a gold medal for the Herend Porcelain Factory. The County Assembly organized a reception for Fischer at which he was fêted and presented with scrolls of honour.[31]

In the years following the fire, there was a revolutionary change in factory policy. The foreign factories were flooding the market with everyday utensils, so the factory stopped producing them. Fischer saw clearly that he was going to be able to sell only high quality goods in the foreign markets. He would therefore have to compete with the elaborate, highly decorative porcelain produced in Meissen, Sèvres, Capo di Monte and Vienna. There was keen competition between all the well-known European factories, but for Herend success was a matter of survival. Little by little Herend began to dominate the home market. János Erdélyi gave expression to the trend in "Our National Industry in 1843" where he wrote: "Since Móric Fischer became owner of the Herend Porcelain Factory there has been every hope that our home-produced translucent tableware would be recognized for its exceptional beauty and durability."

Meissen had also been the chief influence in most of the other factories, not only because it had been founded earlier than any other factory, but also because of its imaginative spirit. The wide variety of forms and types of decoration seen on Meissen porcelain inspired many European factories to emulate the Meissen style. In this few of them were as successful as Herend, which drew on the expertise of foreign craftsmen who settled in Hungary. There was a shortage of skilled modellers who might have contributed individuality to Herend's traditional forms. This explains why during these years Herend manufactured mainly tea and coffee services. Very few figurines were made.

The Meissen heritage was mainly in the field of decoration. Herend tableware now adopted basket-weaving and relief-borders with the typical Meissen bouquet as a central motif on plates, also used on tea-caddies and soup tureens. This Meissen motif is very prominent on the soup tureen of a service dating from the 1840s. The central

24

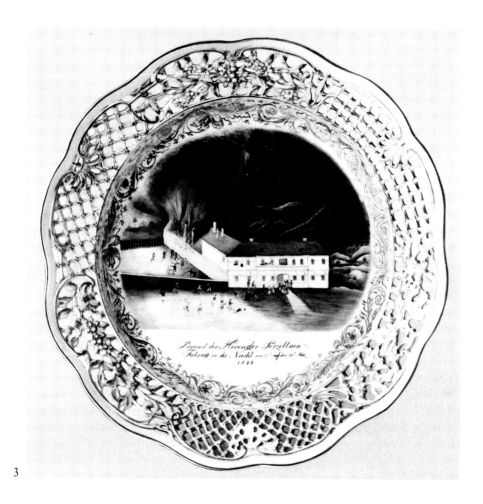

3

multi-coloured bouquet is surrounded by a scattering of tiny sprays of flowers. The handle of the tureen-lid is in the form of a halved lemon, the handles of the tureen being formed in the shape of twisting, root-like branches. The flower-motif and the root-like form of the handles is frequently found, sometimes with interesting adaptations, on dessert-bowls and decorative trays.

All these features have survived and can still be seen on contemporary porcelain made at Herend—the open work borders and the realistic paintings of roses, strawberries and lemon halves. The popular reproductions of peaches, plums and pears are all adaptation of original Meissen motifs.

The porcelain painters at Herend were also glad to adopt the Meissen style in their reproductions of birds with multicoloured plumage; and as porcelain-painting was frequently an inherited occupation, a Herend tradition developed in respect to this art. This is exemplified in the series of twelve types of multicoloured birds depicted in a variety of ways, singing, perched in a tree, or in pairs surrounded by tiny insects, all painted in mellow pastel shades and in a naturalistic way. The minuteness of the scale in which the birds are depicted reflects the French taste. It is a design much favoured by the Rotschild family and is therefore known as the "Rotschild bird" design.

In the original Meissen motif, "Saxe oiseaux", the birds are bigger, and there is a charming naïveté in the style. This motif has also been adopted at Herend and it is still being used.[32]

The painters of Herend freely adapted their heritage of Meissen motifs, creating more local and Hungarian versions, introducing imaginative representations of the wild flowers seen in the Bakony mountain. Sometimes they simplified the Meissen design, sometimes they stressed one particular motif. In this way they created the popular Apponyi-design. "Fleurs des Indes" originated in India, and was much used on English earthenware. This was in fact the source of inspiration for the painters at Meissen who later sold the design to the Old Vienna factory, under the name "Indian Flower", or "Indian Basket". The variation developed by the Herend painters comes closest to the Meissen design. The stylized flowers growing rampant over the flower baskets are undoubtedly of Indian origin.[33]

The design was simplified to suit the taste of the Apponyi family, so that it consisted of a central stylized flower and a border of scattered flower motifs and garlands, enriched with touches of gold.

Another development was the "Vieux Bouquet de Saxe", one of the most important of the Herend designs. It comprises a bouquet of flowers, depicted in stronger colours and very firmly outlined, thus giving a richer and more decorative effect than the "Bouquet de Saxe". It includes both garden and wild flowers. The origin of the motif can be traced back to 1857 when it was used to decorate a dinner service in the baroque style. The painting, technique and overall effect reflects the combined influence of Meissen and Altwien.[34] It is now being gradually replaced by the newer "Bouquet de Tulipe" design.

Herend was influenced by Sèvres to a lesser degree. Two designs adopted from Sèvres are those featuring lattice work with flower motifs and the shepherd scenes painted on an enclosed white ground on light blue coffee services. The water fowl and golden pheasants for chimney-piece shelves made during the seventies are also adopted from Sèvres.

One of the most beautiful mementos of their influence is the "Sèvres Petites Roses" coffee service in the Empire style. This is the gay and elegant design incorporating roses and leaves placed within a gilded trellised field.

Viennese shapes are reflected in Herend vases made in the Empire style. They show a wide variation from the original. The Alpine flower design is directly inspired by a design from Vienna which comprises cyclamen, heather and edelweiss, as well as by the realistic Viennese bouquet and the parsley design which is enchanting just because of its simplicity. Sometimes the plates and dishes are decorated only by a border of parsley, while others are given a more elaborate design in which garlands of claspers are interwoven with stylized heads of parsley. The plates with parsley

4

patterns were originally made with a plain border and on most of them we find the lattice effect. The centre of the plate is plain except for a scattering of parsley leaves. This was Franz Joseph's favourite design, and after the closedown of the Old Vienna Factory, he gave it to Herend.

The immense popularity during the first half of the nineteenth century of the Vienna "Petites Roses" design stimulated artists at Herend to make use of it. Their design consisted of small roses and rosebuds distributed evenly along borders lacquered with purple, later with gold. For many decades it was the design most favoured by the Vienna Court and by the Austrian distributors of Herend.[35]

The artistry of the new Herend porcelain brought renown to the factory. The Hungarian nobility patronized Herend whenever they wished to supplement the foreign services they had inherited. Fischer was right to think that he had nothing to fear from foreign competition. He never relaxed his search for ways by which to improve the quality and appearance of his products. Countess Colonna, in *Les Arts en Europe,* commented on developments at Herend: "The imitation of beautiful old pieces of foreign origin is something no other manufacturer has had the courage to attempt."[36]

Count Károly Esterházy's wife started this trend in 1844 when she ordered from Herend individual pieces to replace those missing from her Meissen service. The pieces delivered by Fischer were almost exact copies of the originals. There followed more orders from aristocratic families—Batthyány, Pálffy, Zichy and Széchenyi. The fame of Herend was established, the reputation of the factory secured. Herend porcelain was acknowledged in Vienna itself when, in 1845, at the Viennese Industrial Exhibition, Herend received an honourable mention for its imitations of early Meissen. This award signalled a spate of orders for every kind of "Meissen" tableware. Fischer

27

5

reported to the newspaper *Hon* that when he was in Dresden he had been given
certain Meissen pieces by the supplier to the Court who asked him to make copies.[37]
This success in the realm of design did not halt Fischer's interest in technical innovation and through all these years he remained firmly in control of the marketing and
financial arrangements.

Aware as he was of the enormous cost of expansion, Fischer turned to Count Károly
Esterházy, ever an enthusiastic benefactor of the factory, and with his support, sought
from the House of Rotschild in Paris a loan of 25,000 silver forints, repayable over
a period of several years. His application succeeded. Baron Rotschild agreed to the
loan, asking only that Esterházy should be the guarantor.[38] The wisdom of borrowing this vast sum was amply confirmed by the subsequent history of the factory.

In 1846 the nation prepared to launch a third Industrial Exhibition. Funds were raised
by means of a raffle, the prize being "a tea service made at Móric Fischer's Herend
Porcelain Factory, with appropriate linen made by Patricz Wiethner, master-weaver
of Győr".

Herend porcelain was once again judged worthy of a gold medal. In his speech

28

Kossuth said to the Herend craftsmen that their present achievement was a "pledge of better times to come". But the "better times" turned out to be not days of peaceful industrial growth, but days of struggle for social reform and for a free and independent Hungarian industry.

The growth of the factory ran parallel to the age of revolution. Kossuth had always supported Fischer. Fischer had experienced first hand the frustrations inherent in the feudal legacy. When he bought the factory site, he had been obliged to challenge the law of entail. His contract stated that: "Since the above purchaser, by virtue of his destiny, according to the laws of the country, is not entitled to own noble property … I am maintaining … my right as a landlord … and for this, I exact the sum of 1 forint."

We can therefore appreciate Fischer's attitude to the events on March 15, 1848, reported as follows to the Sub-Prefect by Lajos Szalonkay, Chief Justice: "Honourable First Sub-Prefect! News of last night's events in Vienna and Pozsony, as announced by Fischer of Herend in Pápa, have so roused the enthusiasm of our citizens that this evening a lawyer by the name of Lazar, accompanied by a college student went to the city judge and demanded that all citizens illuminate their windows."[39] While his sons were fighting in the army of 1848, Fischer was fighting for the continued existence of his factory.

The correspondence between the Herend factory and the first independent ministry is very instructive. It provides details of production, working capital, labour relations and certain as yet obscure artistic issues. It also helps us to understand some of the manifold efforts of government during the War of Independence.

In the middle of 1848 Fischer reported to the Ministry of Industry and Commerce that because of the revolutionary situation, he could neither sell his goods nor provide working capital to continue production unless the government provided him with a loan of 3,000 forints. He offered stock worth 4,500 forints, stored in the Handicrafts Warehouse in Pest as security.

From Fischer's petition to the ministry we learn that in 1848 the factory's workforce totalled 36, and that throughout the year he employed approximately 14 casual workers every day. Capital reserves amounted to 35,000 forints. He produced 50,000 pieces of merchandise per year, worth approximately 20,000 forints. Goods ranged from sweet-jars to 26 inch high vases costing 200 forints.

Fischer was satisfied with production, also with sales amounting to 4,000 a year, handled by the Handicraft Warehouse in Pest. But he had been obliged to lower prices by as much as ten per cent in order to compete with substandard foreign goods imported without payment of duty. The situation obliged him to: "adhere to the traditional 'Saxon' styles and designs now returning to popularity". Few other factories were willing to do this, so the way was open, the only way, for Herend to remain competitive without lowering its prices.

Fischer included in his report an interesting comment on the conceit of the foreign workers who, knowing that they are indispensable, have banded together to disobey shop rules. "...They are so strongly united for the protection of their own interests, that not even the meekest would take a step on his own initiative." In order to break this dangerous solidarity Fischer planned new workshops in which it would be possible to segregate the various areas of production.

Fischer was also looking to future developments in the Hungarian ceramics industry. He suggested that the government should not permit the concentration of one industry in any given area, pointing out that such expansion would exhaust local resources, such as wood and minerals—the very reason for the foundation of the original factory. He also suggested that factories should be exempt from making contributions for building roads and bridges, land tax, road and bridge tolls. Fischer illustrated the inequity of the system by the fact that transport costs between Herend and Csákberény (c. 60 km) were the same as between Vienna and Herend (c. 220 km). Meantime, Imre Garay, director of the Handicraft Warehouse was being asked by the Ministry of Commerce to submit more information about the Herend stock offered as security against the loan. His inventory provides valuable information. There were, for instance, several 12-person tea services in both the Esterházy and the Zay designs, teapots in the national colours and a large selection of vessels decorated with the Viennese parsley-design; also heavily gilded vases and candelabra, Turkish pipes, pastry trays, and holy-water basins, etc.

The National Defence Committee, then acting as the government, did not ignore Fischer's appeal in spite of their extraordinarily critical situation. However, there were some ministers who did not wish to grant the loan and who reported in these terms: "The applicant's goods cannot be classified as essential, especially in our present war economy ... considering that porcelain manufacture even in industrially more advanced countries has to be supported by the state or by public funds ... I advise against granting a loan to this applicant."[40]

THE GOLDEN YEARS

1851–1873

From around 1850 conditions throughout Europe favoured a return to the style of porcelain manufactured more than a hundred years previously. This trend was supported by the prosperity of the bourgeoisie, a class that expanded with the development of the industrial revolution. The trend was characterized by an urge to recover past traditions, but eventually it resulted in a complete falling away from reality. While in the arts generally the trend was to look backwards, in the porcelain industry all eyes were turned to the East. Thus the oriental designs produced at Herend were admirably suited to contemporary taste.

Mid-nineteenth century Herend designs were undoubtedly developed in imitation of the oriental scenes painted on old pieces of porcelain provided by members of the aristocracy for copying.[41] But the Herend painters were not merely copiers, they tried to emulate the early techniques while creating new forms and designs.[42]

Fischer recorded the necessary equipments: "This particular glaze (July 12) survived the firing without melting, nor did it melt after a firing lasting 22 hours."[43]

It would be in vain to search for any specific source of inspiration for the Herend style. In Hungary, most branches of art have been influenced by the West. It could not be otherwise in a country that had been isolated for centuries. The Herend contribution to the art of ceramics was to assimilate outside influences, adapt them and add an individual note that was truly Hungarian. It was a notable achievement merely to reproduce the essential paste necessary for porcelain manufacture, and to copy the glaze and the colours. Later they enriched this heritage by creating highly individual motifs and designs. Their achievement in the fields of art and technology was first recognized during the successive world exhibitions inaugurated in 1851.

The idea of a world exhibition was first conceived by Prince Albert, husband of Victoria, the Queen of England. "Gentlemen—the Exhibition of 1851 is to give us a true test and a living picture of the point of development at which the whole of mankind has arrived ... and a new starting-point from which all nations will be able to direct their further exertions. I confidently hope that the impression which the view of this vast collection will produce upon the spectator will be ... the conviction that they can only be realized in proportion to the help which we are prepared to render each other; therefore, only by peace, love, and ready assistance, not only between individuals, but between the nations of the earth."[44]

When the Great Exhibition was opened in 1851 at the Crystal Palace, London, fourteen thousand eight hundred and thirty-one exhibitors demonstrated to the general public, the finest achievements known in the realms of industry, art and science.

The exhibit of Herend porcelain was a first step to world-wide recognition of the factory which was thus freed from its long association with the name of Vienna. According to one of the guides: "The beautiful vases, dinner, tea and coffee services exhibited by Mr. Móric Fischer (Herend, near Veszprém, Hungary) were admired by all who visited the exhibition. Here is porcelain of the very best quality and design."

Fischer was especially proud of his Old-Meissen vases and a tray bordered with Chinese motifs and with a representation of Maria Theresa with Hungarian aristocrats in the famous scenes of "vitam and sanguinem".[45]

It was at this exhibition that Queen Victoria of England ordered a dinner service decorated with the Chinese design of butterflies and flowers. The "Queen Victoria", also known as the "Victoria" design is still one of the most popular of the Herend factory. It comprises sprays of flowers and butterflies, painted in the full range of the Herend colours. Decorative in the extreme and enriched by local innovations, it is peculiarly Hungarian in character.

Although the factory was not officially represented and the porcelain was exhibited as the product of an Austrian factory, Herend porcelain was awarded a first class medal (Exhibition of Industrial Products of all Nations. Prize medal). [46] All the exhibits were sold and orders were received from the Duke of Westminster, the Princess of Teck, Sir Robert Wallace, the Duke of Westmoreland and many other British notabilities.[47]

Fischer tried to take advantage of his success in London but he was now mainly interested in the artistic aspects of porcelain and he neglected the possibilities for technical innovation and improved marketing. It was important to improve the quality of his products but it was equally important to promote them. For him it was enough that he had commissioned Lipót Fischer, factory representative, to negotiate sales in Bohemia and Germany, while he himself transformed the first storey of the family home in Tata so that goods could be displayed and sold there.[48]

Having repaid the Rotschild loan, Fischer now sought government assistance; but although all the large European factories were government sponsored, Fischer's application was rejected.

Nevertheless, Herend porcelain was reaching the foreign markets, and in 1853, at the International Industrial Exhibition in New York it was awarded the first prize. On the first day of the exhibition, the President of the United States, Franklin Pierce, purchased several pieces of Herend porcelain, and on the second day, the Austrian consul reported to his government that all the exhibited articles had been sold.[49] Though gratified by this success, Fischer knew that this was no moment for relaxation of effort. In 1853 the Chamber of Pest–Buda published its annual report in which it was revealed that turnover in the porcelain industry had fallen by fifty per cent. The Chamber attributed this to high food prices, wage increases and the long prevailing war in the East. Herend's most lucrative domestic market was being flooded with inexpensive Czech and Viennese porcelain.[50]

Fischer looked for trade by means of another world exhibition. His hopes were centred on Paris for it was the French who were the first to follow the British example by organizing another exhibition based on the successful Great Exhibition of 1851.[51] Herend's contribution to the Great Paris Exhibition in 1855[52] was again a selection of Chinese-porcelain imitations. The comment in *Pester Lloyd* was that, of the Hungarian industrial products exhibited in Paris, "the Chinese-porcelain imitations of Mr. Fischer of Herend take first place. Even experts are deceived by the cups and dishes. In colour, form and quality, they are counterparts of the Chinese originals. One particularly fine tea service is now in the possession of Her Imperial Royal Highness Princess Sophie, who received it as a Christmas gift from her son, the Emperor."[53] All the exhibits were bought by members of the aristocracy. Fischer was present to receive his high award.

Fischer's name is certainly inseparable from the factory's many successes, as these would not have been possible without his brilliant gift for organization, his refined artistic taste and his foresight. But the fame of Herend also depended to a large extent on the loyal and zealous contribution of the factory workforce. These were the craftsmen who helped Fischer to carry out his experiments, to control the kilns, to implement his designs, many of them making individual creative innovations—and sometimes, as we may see in the yellow pages of old cash books—providing financial assistance, even though their wages varied according to the state of the factory balance sheet. We therefore record here the names of some of these foot-soldiers of industry mentioned in the accounts for 1858: painters Aue, Branald, Eckart, Fischer, Friedl, Fritsch, Hofhansel, Kemplies, Kutschera, Kohut, Marschak, Novák, Schniegler, Simon, Stôbler, Tehierl, Trojanek, Werner and Zitt; polishers Mrs. Fischer and Mrs. Schmiedel; apprentice painters Antal and Pál; moulder Vogel; modelmaker Lőwy; wheelers Fritch, Jungnitsch, Münzl and Joppe, and kiln operators Mészáros and Takács. Other kiln operators were given only Christian names: Pál, Sándor, Johann, Imre, József, Anti, while there were casemakers by the name of Takács, Pál and Pista. In addition to this listing we wish to record the name of Ede Varsányi, painter, who is credited with the most beautiful porcelain paintings of the era.

We can see from the names that most of the workers were of foreign birth, the "migrant birds" once mentioned by Kossuth. Monthly wages for kiln operators amounted to between 13–18 forints, for painters 10–13 forints. Simon had the highest

6

pay, 33–36 forints. He was probably the chief painter. The wages of the moulders are recorded as about 20 forints.[54] These lists constitute the earliest known record of factory workers in Hungary.

Factory production was stimulated by the publicity resulting from the Paris Exhibition award, though even before the opening of the exhibition, Herend had received a gold medal from the Belgian king. An international jury, presided over by Prince Napoleon, acting as president of the Imperial Committee, pronounced as follows: "The factory of Mr. Móric Fischer contains only two kilns, and his yearly turnover is merely 70,000 forints. Mr. Fischer's exhibits contain mainly imitations of Chinese and Japanese porcelain, but these are worthy of attention from every standpoint. The execution is exquisite, and the decoration is applied with a high degree of intelligence and good taste."[55]

In 1857 another tribute arrived from the natural scientist Alexander von Humboldt when he thanked the factory for a gift of porcelain to mark his 88th birthday.[56] The signed photograph accompanying his letter is treasured in the factory museum. The factory produced a twenty inch high porcelain relief portrait based on this photograph, coloured brown and gold on a white background and bearing the scientist's tribute: "Your imitations of the Chinese—in delicacy of form, colouring and style— comes closer to the originals than anything I have ever seen. Your relief work, your cups, plates, vases and pierced designs all equally deceive the eye, and my gratitude is as genuine as the respect I feel for the noble and fortunate man who thus adds to the artistry of industrial activity. Alexander v. Humboldt – Potsdam, Oct. 1857."

In this way the standard of Herend porcelain improved in response to the appreciation

6

of visitors to exhibitions and with every improvement Herend porcelain found new markets. It was now an axiom that orders for replacement of old Chinese or Sèvres pieces always found their way to Herend whether needed by European royalty or by the inhabitants of Petersburg, Moscow, Lisbon or Naples.

Success, however, brought no diminution of Fischer's expansionary projects. After several rejections, he was granted in 1857 a loan from the Industrial and Commercial Credit Institute in Vienna of 40,000 forints, which enabled him to increase production to such an extent that in the course of ten years the value of the factory rose from 70,000 forints to 400,000 forints.[57]

After only three years, in 1860, the Pest–Buda Chamber of Commerce and Industry reported that factory personnel had increased by twenty, the total number of employees being now sixty, of whom twenty were painters, four kiln operators and wheelers, and eight "dough makers" (those who prepared the basic paste).[58] The rhythm of production, now independent of foreign competition, was firmly established by the early sixties. Essentially the goal was to modernize the factory. It was necessary to acquire the best possible raw materials as cheaply as possible and to make the best use of them by employing the most advanced methods. The first task was therefore to extend the factory buildings, buy new kilns and grinding equipment and keep abreast of all technological developments in the industry. Only then would it be possible to satisfy an expanding market, and fulfil orders on time. The artistic standards maintained in the majority of porcelain factories had until this time been dependent on individual work by hand. At Herend, all the porcelain was shaped and painted by hand. The wheelers moulded by hand large plates, tea caddies and coffee cans, glued on the legs, finishing, with hand tools, even the rims. They used their

EXHIBITION·OF·THE·WORKS·OF·INDUSTRY·
OF·ALL·NATIONS·1851·

I hereby certify that Her Majestys Commissioners
upon the Award of the Jurors have presented a Prize Medal to

Herr Moritz Fischer

for Porcelain

shewn in the Exhibition

Exhibition

le Paul London 15th Oct 1851

Albert

Pres. of the Royal Commission

hands as well as a shovel when mixing the paste. Today all these processes are carried out by power-driven machines.[59]

Fischer's application to the Chamber of Commerce and Industry indicates conditions at Herend around 1850. The firing was done in three French-made, wood-heated kilns. Heavy loads had to be levered into position. The supply of cheap but satisfactory kaolin and clay was a constant problem. Fischer suggested the re-opening of the kaolin mines of Zólyom county, Radvány and others to the north of Ungvár (now Užgorod, Soviet Union). He believed that once iron content had been removed, this kaolin would be as good as the kaolin from Limoges. He also mentioned that good quality feldspar, granite and quartz was available in the vicinity of Graz. Probably he had already used it, since in the forties he had complained that it was impossible to produce pure white porcelain from the local quartz. Fischer's analysis of production costs makes interesting reading. Kaolin was the most expensive of the necessary materials at 6 forints for 100 lb.; the other two essentials were fire-proof clay, 25 fillér (100 lb.) wood, 20 fillér for 100 lb. Thus one fired plate using $\frac{1}{3}$ lbs kaolin at 2 fillérs, 8 lb. fireproof clay ($\frac{8}{100}$ lb.) at 2 fillérs, 20 lb. firewood at 4 fillérs, was produced for a total of 8 fillérs. The same plate fired in Pest would have cost 30 fillérs. Fischer also stated that the cost of kaolin was not of prime importance; since it was imported, the price was the same everywhere. The determining factor in the cost of porcelain was the price of wood and fire-proof clay, both of which were used in large quantities. These were both available cheaply in the vicinity of Herend. Living conditions were better in Herend than elsewhere, attracting skilled workers from abroad.[60]

During the golden years of the plant, between 1851 and 1873, artistic activities at Herend were twofold, first to continue the replacement or completion of old services[61] which provided a solid economic base, the other to create new pieces inspired by the old Oriental porcelains.

The second objective involved a determined rejection of a decadent contemporary style and also scientific experiments to discover the kind of paste, colours and firing methods used but long forgotten even by their original creators, the Chinese. Although the factory adopted the forms and design-motifs of the old, Far Eastern porcelain, it transformed them into the unique style of Herend.

Fischer's artistic aims were published in the press:

"During the last few decades, throughout the procelain industry, manufacturers have abandoned the early shapes and designs which have been passed down to us. Even at Sèvres and Meissen there has been a slavish attempt to follow the dictates of fashion. My own policy, however, has always been to learn from the past, from those factories which at the height of their glory produced the most beautiful porcelain. I refer of course to the Chinese and the Japanese under the Emperors Hun and Ming; Sèvres in the era of Louis XV; and Meissen and Frankenthal during the reign of Augustus the Strong and Karl Theodor. I have been helped in this endeavour by the fact that several of our noble gentlemen, who, because of the original factories' departure from the old styles, were unable to complete their inherited art treasures, have entrusted me with this task ... large orders have been placed with us, others are still coming in, which I am barely able to fulfil... In my patriotic efforts I have prominently displaced my emblem on every one of my products and I have proudly stamped on them Hungary's coat of arms with the letters MF and the name of Herend. Encouraged by my success, and prompted by a number of experts, I have decided—as I have already told M. Roy and other gentlemen when I spoke at the banquet of the 1855 Paris Exhibition—that in the future I shall use on my products not the humble 'after vieux Sèvres' or 'after vieux Saxe' but the original Herend emblem. In fact I have nurtured an independent Herend style, and I will adhere to it. Therefore I believe, that if the imitating of any genre deserves reproof, then I may reprove Meissen—whom I indirectly re-oriented to their old style—as 'Herend imitators'." Fisher was expressing a truth exemplified by the creations produced in the factory during this period and which marked a renaissance of the art of porcelain-manufacture. Together with the craftsmen, wheelers and painters of Herend, he was rescuing from oblivion a forgotten art and offering to the public the new eclectic yet individual style of Herend.

The influence of Sèvres and Meissen was evident, but from the middle of the fifties it was the Far-Eastern style that dominated the Herend experiment. In the early sixties, Hungarian peasant scenes began to appear, as for instance the genre scene on a coffee service made in 1862. Several figurines, also animal figures, date from this

7

8

9

period—including for example the "Large Chinese Fish", or the "Seated Turkish Man and Woman".

The most valued relics of the artistic creations of these years are the vases and services incorporating Chinese motifs. These show exquisite workmanship in the highly imaginative detail, bizarre forms and colour harmonies. It would be hard to select any of these products for particular praise. Some we admire for the painting of the figures, so perfectly expressing movement—perhaps by means of only one or two strokes of the brush. On others we may appreciate the stylized flowers so carefully placed, or the rich yet never overbearing gold ornamentation. Each design has its own charm, the earliest being the Victoria design mentioned earlier and the Ming, Gödöllő and Esterházy designs.

The "Ming" design, in which figures are encircled by richly gilded garlands, evolved around the middle of the nineteenth century. Centrally placed in this design is the figure of a seated woman depicted in a Chinese setting, the colours being typical of Chinese porcelain. In the foreground are male Chinese figures. The design is often found on tea services. The enamel technique was used for the motif, gold leaf for the borders. There is a very fine example of this type of decoration on a plate dated 1868, now in the museum at Debrecen. The border features a reticulated oval beehive shape, outlined in gold and with turquoise glaze. The inner edge of the border is delicately outlined in red.[62] Legend has it that this design is connected with the Sardian Court. When the need arose to replace some of the pieces, it was found that none of the European factories could undertake the task, though Count Revel, the King's ambassador approached numerous factories before hearing of Herend where Fischer at

last accepted the commission. After a year of experiment Fischer produced a suitable paste and glaze and he personally delivered the finished pieces. So confident was he of the quality of his porcelain that he secretly abstracted a number of the original pieces on display, substituting his own products. When he confessed the ruse, his pieces were the more appreciated.[63]

In 1864, in the *Wiener Abendpost,* an article on Herend porcelain commented on the Herend copies of the "Ming" design: "The colours of the cup belong to the so-called 'Ming' design, where certain scenes are depicted in specified colours, as was the custom in the twelfth century. Each colour requires a different temperature of the kiln, a difficulty which finally caused the Chinese to abandon the 'Ming' design. At Herend copies of the "Ming" design: "The colours of the cup belong to the so-called reproduction of the 'Ming' design. From this cup an expert can tell that Mr. Fischer knows every aspect of his trade."[64]

The "Miramare" design was created in the mid-nineteenth century for the Miramare castle owned by the ill-fated Maximilian, Emperor of Mexico. The painting, in under-glaze cobalt, depicts in the foreground a fruit-laden tree and a building resembling a watchtower, in the background a pagoda and ruins. The gilding and garlands give an effect of richness which is in no way excessive.

The "Gödöllő" design (Gödöllő was the summer residence of the Hungarian king)

was developed in the early 1850s, after an original Chinese cup now in the museum of Herend. Even the subsidiary motifs are elaborate, the overall effect being very oriental, with stylized tree-trunks and flower motifs in *sang-de-boeuf*. The original Chinese design is accented by the addition of handles in the form of mandarin figures, and certain other stylistic modifications. Because of the geometric precision with which the base-lines are drawn it is one of the most decorative of the Chinese-type designs. It was first called "Sang Rouge" and later changed to "Gödöllő", when Franz Joseph presented it to his wife, Queen Elizabeth, for the royal palace in Gödöllő. Where the base-lines are painted in yellow, the design is known as "Sang Jaune" or "Yellow Sang".

The "Esterházy" design was adapted from porcelain brought to Hungary around the mid-nineteenth century by a member of Prince Esterházy's family, who was ambassador in St. Petersburg. It consists of a simple stylized sedge-flower design, originally scraped out of a brick-red base, with Chinese characters, all in white, clearly defined against the brick-red or dark green background. Certain motifs of the original Chinese "Cubash" design had already been used by the earthenware factory at Holics. The stylized "Famille Rose", cleverly placed on a neutral background decorated with brownish-grey spirals, has a charming naïveté. The trays and cups are bordered with spiralled garlands in gilt, enlivening an otherwise simple background.

It is essentially a Chinese creation, but the stylization is already typical of Herend. It was first produced in Herend for Count Cubash of London. Herend's version of a Chinese design closely adapted to the European taste is the "Windsor Castle". Centrally placed on the plates we find once again the "Famille Rose", the stylized Chinese rose, bordered by liane-like flowers painted in brick-red and lilac. The first service was commissioned in the sixties for Windsor Castle, home of the British royal family.

One of the richest and most decorative of the Herend designs is the "Black Sang" or "Sang Noir". Stylistically, because of the geometric arrangement, it is quite closely related to the "Gödöllő" design, but the Chinese roses and flowers within the rectangular fields are different. Here the liane, shown growing through flowers on a black ground, gives to the design its unique charm. It is used to decorate tea and coffe services as well as purely ornamental pieces.

The figural "Tschung" design reflects the wealth of the Chinese heritage—which is similarly perpetuated by the "Macao" design comprising stylized birds on a black background. The latter is used primarily for the decoration of ornamental porcelain pieces.

The "Fish" or "Poissons" design closely follows, in both colouring and form, the old Chinese porcelain. The blue-grey ground is in keeping with the essentially Chinese style of the design. The effect is highly decorative, being painted in blue, *sang-de-boeuf*, white and gold between patches of green seaweed, blue garlands and plants outlined in black.

We find the "Fish" design in pleasant combinations on the double-walled ornamental trays and cups. Franz Joseph purchased a service of this type at the Vienna Exhibition for presentation to the Prince of Wales, later King Edward VII. The design was thereafter named "Wales".

The manufacture of these services and beer mugs of similar design, required careful supervision. The walls of each piece consist of two parts, a smooth inner wall and an outer shell of delicately-pierced porcelain. The snake-shaped handles, the gilded bands dividing the lace-like fields, the oriental garlands and a lavish application of gilt, all contribute to the effect of splendour.

In the *Wiener Post* there is a reference to examples of this type of Herend featuring an outer shell of pierced porcelain now in an Austrian museum: "The most advanced technology is required for the manufacture of this cup on high legs, and a pot, both with an outer shell of porcelain pierced like a grate. It appears to have been made in one piece; there are no screws or staples made of any other foreign material. The outer wall is attached to the solid inner wall of porcelain at the rim and at the base. When we asked Mr. Fischer how he was able to prevent cracking and how he was able to paint one wall behind the other he shrugged and said that is *his* secret, he cannot disclose it."[65]

Another superb example of the artistic and technological standards prevailing at

Herend is an 1851 ornamental vase painted by Ede Varsányi. On one side there is a portrait of Fischer, on the other a view of the factory—a meticulous architectural drawing. Elaborately moulded, wreathed in gilt, this vase is in the baroque style which appealed to the contemporary taste. Similar virtuosity is demonstrated in the two-eared vase with a portrait of Prince Albert.

The figurine of a Chinese boy with a fish dates back to the 1860s. We assume it to be the work of a foreign artist since it features only Chinese elements, with no trace of Hungarian influence. The belief that he was one of Herend's "migrating birds" is confirmed by the fact that we know of no other figurines dating from this period. The fish is larger than the Chinese child, whose body is aligned to the vertically placed fish. The structure and anatomic shaping suggest that it was modelled from life. The face of the child is less expressive. He is shown wearing a rust-coloured head-dress, a yellow kimono with splashes of other colours and a blue robe with upturned sleeves. The eyes and the mouth of the sea-green fish are exaggerated. The sea is suggested by the blue-green and purple colouring of the base.

Among the Herend masterpieces of this period are the approximately 20 inch high Japanese/Chinese-style vases. These are either beautifully enamelled or decorated with green cobalt-glaze. We should also mention a vase which has been in a museum in Austria since 1873. The solid base has mounts at each corner in the shape of standing lions, with movable chains in their mouths made of one piece of porcelain. A closed hand is encircled by each handle. The sides of the vase are painted and are enclosed in an outer shell of pierced porcelain. The handle is an exact replica of the Hungarian crown.

The two-tier fruit stand made in 1861 is clearly influenced by Sèvres. The undulating edges of the stand and both trays are richly decorated, bands of motifs separated by gilt lines. Spaced along these opulent Empire-style borders are medallions outlined in gold. The inner part of the stand is strewn with cornflowers and sprays of roses. A screwed-in, circular handle with relief decoration protrudes from the upper part of the stand.[66]

The products of the 1850s and 1860s reflect, in both form and design, the continuing tradition of Meissen. The samovar made for the court of the Czar is an interesting and beautiful piece from the period. A duplicate is on display in the Herend museum. The moulded female figures used for handles and the fish placed in the centre enliven the otherwise relatively simple form.

With these superb creations, Herend satisfied contemporary taste and met the growing demand for porcelain. It achieved world-wide recognition not only for the Herend factory, but for Hungarian industry as a whole. The craftsmen of Herend were always ready to experiment, in art as in technology, in the choice of raw materials, the use of paint, the methods of firing.[67]

The individuality of the Herend style was described by Professor Diebitsch: "The imitation of even the simplest flower cannot be called mere copying, every motif has its own individuality and is imbued with the naive charm of the Herend artist who was once a peasant boy."[68]

The 1862 World Exhibition in London added once again to the reputation of Herend. According to the *Luzerner Neueste Nachrichten,* the Herend exhibit was a thin porcelain plate, 1 metre in diameter, an imitation of Chinese "Celadon", and the world's largest known porcelain object in existence at the time. The design, already produced at Herend, depicted Maria Theresa with her son in her arms, with Hungarian noblemen forming a semi-circle around them.[69]

A year later, in 1863, Lothar Bucher, reporting the 1863 exhibition in London again commented on the skill with which Fischer produced such perfect imitations of fine Chinese porcelain. In his judgment, Fischer's Chinese green came closer to the original than anything from Sèvres. The factory was awarded the prestigious "Honoris causa" medal.[70]

Herend's success had its own echo at home. The *Vasárnapi Újság* published a leading article about the factory, along with a picture of Fischer. Of the London exhibition they wrote: "At last year's industrial art exhibition, Chinese-type porcelain dishes from Herend were the centre of attention."

On February 21, 1863 Fischer was presented to the Emperor, and in recognition of his success in London, he received a Franz Joseph Order of Knighthood. In 1864 the Imperial Porcelain Factory was closed because of lack of business and Herend received the rights to the protected patents.

Then just as production and reputation alike were soaring, Fischer had to face another catastrophe. Fire broke out again in the factory, and even the recently built façade fell victim to the flames. The story of 1843 was repeated: the ruins were cleared away and the factory rebuilt, production was recommenced and the standard of work once again received recognition when Herend was awarded an honourable mention in 1865 at an industrial exhibition held in Pozsony.

Meanwhile France, anxious to let the world see the glorious achievements of the empire, was busy keeping alive the idea of another exhibition. Since France was now a powerful nation, she could afford to do so. Nevertheless, it had to be recognized that a mere repeat-performance of the last world fair would not satisfy the public. The Paris Exhibition of 1867 was therefore organized round a novel theme—the history of work, working tools and products.

The Austrian authorities invited Hungarian representatives of industry to assist in the selection of exhibits. It was inconceivable that Fischer should not be one of them. Committees were formed to represent the individual branches of industry and Mór Fischer's name appeared in the list of representatives[71] drawn up by the Governor General and announced on December 18, 1865: "... in accordance with the gracious order of the Court, and in the interest of having our nation duly represented at the World Exhibition in Paris in 1867, a national committee has been formed as fol-

lows..." The list included Fischer, which was not only an honour for him, but for Herend as well.

The location chosen for the Paris Exhibition was the champs de Mars, a setting which added splendour to the scene quite apart from the novelty of the theme. Public interest was immediately aroused.

The Herend exhibit was much admired and brought with it an unprecedented spate of orders.[73] Account books for 1867—now in the factory's archives—record that between 1865 and 1866 Herend exported to Paris goods worth 1,000 forints, but in the year of the exhibition the value of goods rose to 83,530 forints. In 1868 merchandise worth 10,492,50 forints was exported. In the same year, porcelain, including dinner services, valued at 2,070 forints was sold to Baroness Rotschild. Customers were for the most part members of the aristocracy, but now modest orders were being received from some famous Hungarian politicians and writers, such as Mór Jókai, Ferenc Deák and Baron Miklós Jósika.

The increased volume of sales that followed the exhibition demonstrates that Herend wares were as popular as ever. Mans B. Ducont, a well-known art critic, said briefly: "It is beyond all imagination". The *Wiener Zeitung* added more explicitly: "Mór Fischer of Herend has upheld his reputation even in Paris. He surpasses even the

Chinese in the imitation of their own old porcelain, but his own creations are just as deserving of credit."

Fischer insisted on delivering only perfect pieces. He inspected everything himself so that he could solve any problem that may have given rise to imperfections. In this way he created his own "Fischer-type" form.[74] Adolphe Thiers—later president of the Republic, who had the reputation of being a discerning art critic and collector —saw the Herend exhibits at the Paris Exhibition where, in Fischer's absence, he left his card with the note: "I have seen Mr. Maurice Fischer's porcelain which I find not only beautiful, but very life-like."[75]

For each exhibition in turn the factory produced a new surprise. In Paris it was the technique that was greeted as "little short of a miracle". The success of the exhibition was assessed in more mundane terms when an offer was made for the factory's models in the sum of 40.000 lb.[76]

The factory received a silver medal, and Fischer was awarded the Officers' Cross of the Legion of Honour. On this occasion the Minister of Justice, Adolphe Crémieux, wrote to Fischer in these terms: "If one compares the old Chinese porcelain objects with those created by your genius, then you are definitely the winner, as you are re-creating the antique works with a perfection as yet unparalleled in art. You have solved the problem of Chinese artistry which, until now, has been judged unattainable. Your success proves the importance of your work. The most outstanding authorities in the field of art, as well as many distinguished notabilities including the King of Hungary and the Empress of France, have demonstrated by their purchases their appreciation of your products—an appreciation well deserved..."[77]

When the Empress of France entertained Franz Joseph and his retinue, she had the table set with Herend porcelain bought at the exhibition.[78]

Nor did the Viennese Court spare its appreciation. When, in recognition of Fischer's activities, Franz Joseph raised him to the nobility, an ambition dear to every citizen was fulfilled. That is when Fischer chose the title "Farkasházy".[79, 80]

Fischer had reached the zenith of his career. Just as in earlier years, when he had not been dismayed by economic difficulties, so now he did not allow himself to be blinded by success. He remained the craftsman who worked regular hours every day of the week. He was an artist struggling for perfection, a manufacturer studying the materials of his trade, experimenting with colour and new manufacturing techniques, ever anxious to maintain and further the fame of Herend. Throughout his life he remained capable of unconventional behaviour, showing little regard for money or purely personal gain. His immediate descendents tell many charming anecdotes of the nonchalance he sometimes displayed in financial matters. One of these anecdotes concerns a dinner service ordered by the Rotschild family. Fischer was so proud of his service that he personally delivered it to Vienna where he found that he had only just enough money to pay the fare. He personally set the table, so that the service appeared to advantage. The Rotschilds were speechless with admiration. Yet when

12

he was offered immediate payment he replied, "When one views a masterpiece, one does not speak of money," and he left. The bill was paid later.

After the festive days of the exhibition Fischer returned to the everyday routine of work, but now he began to delegate more work to his sons. His eldest sons, Leo and Dezső had already gained some experience in the factory. Leo was responsible for the commercial transactions, and often represented the factory abroad; his wife, Katalin, a woman of taste as well as managerial ability, was very active in supervising the employees. Dezső was production manager, responsible for the technical aspects of the production. Vilmos, himself a gifted painter, was in charge of the art department. From 1866, Ignác Fischer—their cousin and brother-in-law—also worked in the factory.

Some idea of life in the factory is revealed in a petition presented by Fischer to the Chamber of Commerce and Industry on February 6, 1867. At that time the factory employed a total workforce of 83 consisting of 22 painters, 10 female gold polishers, 9 wheelers, 5 clay-workers, 8 kiln-operators, 4 people working and grinding the paste, and 25 wood-cutters and day-labourers.[81]

Employees worked from 7 a.m. to 7 p.m. 300 days of the year. The average weekly pay was 300 forints.

The best quality quartz and clay was brought from Northern Hungary, but the coarse quality used for the containers was bought locally. There is very little recorded

47

information about the raw materials used, since Fischer considered that his knowledge of such items as kaolin and paint was a trade secret. According to the catalogue of the Clay and Glass Industrial Exhibition of 1896, Bohemian kaolin was used in Herend since 1840.[82]

In the years following the Paris exhibition, Fischer had to adapt to economic and political changes. After the Compromise of 1867 the door was open to capitalist development in industry.

The early seventies inaugurated an interesting chapter in the history of the factory. For some years after the 1867 Compromise, the ebullient state of the economy was maintained and was reflected in general industrial prosperity. More capital was being invested in industry and new banks and credit institutions were also being established. Success did not come to every industry but one may well find it surprising that there would have been any decline in the fortunes of Herend, well-known for its sound management. Yet it was now that Fischer was obliged to seek outside support. He wrote to the King, the government, sympathetic patrons of the arts, county officials, his friends and various banks and credit institutions. One may equally wonder why it was that his appeals were rejected. After all, his models alone were worth 40,000 forints, which would have served as adequate security.[83]

From 1869 onwards Fischer's requests for loans became more frequent. There were many delays and much procrastination before Fischer's application for 150,000 forints found its way to the Hungarian Landcredit Institute, with recommendations from the ministry. Herend was then visited by a committee of experts headed by Anton I. Hack, a former president of the Imperial Porcelain Factory (now closed down) to study the factory's assets. Hack's sympathetic estimates produced a valuation of 396,207 forints. On the basis of this security, the Hungarian General Landcredit Institution granted a loan of 50,000 forints, which Fischer used to ensure that the factory would participate in the forthcoming exhibition in Vienna in a fashion worthy of its past record. Worried though he must have been, Fischer was prepared for the next world exhibition with his usual enthusiasm.

This time the novelty lay in the choice of a city, for rapidly expanding Vienna was to be the site of the exhibition. But the world economic crisis of 1873 came like thunder out of a blue sky. There were fears that the exhibition would have to be abandoned. Prices fell alarmingly on the Vienna stock exchange, many Austrian and a good number of Hungarian businesses, banks and credit institutions failed. In these depressing circumstances plans for the exhibition continued. When it finally opened, it was greeted with approval on all sides. When it closed, the Austrian authorities were faced with a substantial deficit.

At this exhibition Fischer chose to show porcelain in the "Vieux Herend" style, and his colourful exhibit became the centre of attention despite the fact that the rest of the European ceramics industry was very well represented. On view was a selection of elegant earthenware pieces from England, terracotta from France, charming hard-porcelain wares from Germany and Austria, and many Danish porcelain figurines. This display was described in the *Wiener Weltausstellungs-Zeitung* of October 29, 1873: "We can state without hesitation that nowhere can we see more splendid examples of the art of porcelain than those exhibited in the Hungarian pavilion in the eastern wing of the Palace of Industry. Mr. Móric Fischer displays the unrivalled products of the Herend factory on a pyramid-shaped shelf and in two glass cabinets. A mere passing glance assures us that every object is a museum piece. In conception, colour and execution, there is nothing to equal it in the whole exhibition."[84]

The French delegation praised the variety of the Herend products, pointing out that "this was achieved by Mr. Fischer in spite of the very limited means at his disposal." The Belgian members of the jury pronounced that "the old Japanese vessels of the deepest blue seem to be re-born from their broken fragments, assembled here in all their gaiety in the hands of Mr. Fischer."[85] The factory was awarded the "Medal for Progress" (Fortschrittsmedaille). *Die Weltausstellungs-Zeitung* wrote, "We express the undivided opinion of all the experts when we state that Mr. Fischer merits a far higher award."[86]

The almost daily appearance of one or another illustrious customer was a popular feature of the exhibition. Franz Joseph purchased a table with porcelain legs "à la Chinoise" for presentation to the Czar, also a dinner service for 50, with a dessert service for 50 for the Persian Shah. He purchased a total of 554 pieces as gifts for his guests, among whom were Viktor Emmanuel II, the King of Italy, the Prince of Wales and Carol, King of Romania. Some of the most highly praised pieces were the "Ming" dinner service and a large vase with movable porcelain chains valued by experts at 20,000 forints. The Empress Augusta accompanied Franz Joseph on his visit to the exhibition where she readily recognized some of the Herend pieces she had in her castle and she told the Herend representatives that they were in regular use.[87] On this occasion the factory presented Franz Joseph with a beautiful cobalt-blue ornamental tray with pierced border and gold rim. It is now in the Museum of Applied Arts in Budapest.

Other customers were the Queen of Württemberg, the ruler of Romania and numerous British, French and American notabilities. The factory's success at the exhibition was confirmed by Jakob Falke, a critic of undisputed authority: "Móric Fischer feels no obligation to make imitations of famous pieces of porcelain; he rather prefers to create anew something that is good, beautiful, worthy of admiration... Such a goal can only be achieved through patient deliberation and hard work, especially when we consider the area where the factory is located, far from any possible source of artistic means. This porcelain rightfully claims our admiration... In my opinion Hungary should make more of this factory. With such unique skill at its service, it could bring even greater prestige to the nation and secure markets comparable to those once dominated by Meissen and Vienna."[88]

CRISES AND SURVIVAL

1874–1876

Falke's good advice fell on deaf ears. Government loans were inadequate to save the factory. The effects of the Austrian economic crisis reached Hungary where the porcelain industry suffered an overwhelming change of fortune. The future of the factory was in doubt. Pál Esterházy wrote to Count József Zichy, Minister of Commerce, reminding him of the year 1857, when the factory had been saved by the efforts of his father. The Herend villagers also petitioned the government, citing their contribution as craftsmen and artists. They recorded their own transformation from poor agricultural labourers to the status of skilled industrial craftsmen responsible for the operation of the factory, also the prosperity and material improvements in the village. Closure of the factory would bring about the decay of the village. None of these appeals elicited a government loan.

The letter of rejection from the Ministry arrived in Herend in January 1874. On July 13 of the same year the County of Veszprém called a special meeting to consider Fischer's application for a loan. He was refused in these words: "Notwithstanding the affection felt by the people of the county for the factory of Herend and its famous owners, and their wish to see it continue to prosper, the county is not in a position to grant a loan."[89] They even rejected the factory's request to reduce the county surtax assessment for the year 1874.[90] By the end of the year, the factory company was declared bankrupt.[91]

Without a doubt, the economic crisis of 1873 had contributed to the bankruptcy.[92] Even in 1875 the consequences of the crisis were still being felt, and that in a totally unexpected sphere of the economy, in the credit worthiness of the government itself. It proved detrimental to the economy as a whole, and, along with the negative aspects of the economic administration, it destroyed many of the positive ones as well. Moreover, the government lacked the willingness to render any economic assistance, a willingness that could have saved Herend as it had done, for example, during the War of Independence in 1849.

During these dark days Fischer received the "Sun and Lion Order" fifth-class from the Shah of Persia, and the third-class "Order of Saint Stanislaw" from the Czar of

Russia,[93] while Franz Joseph awarded the gold medal of "Science and Art" for his exhibit at the Vienna exhibition. Fischer looked upon these honours as a last acknowledgement of his past achievements. For his financial difficulties were compounded by the antagonism of his sons. They deplored his concern to make beautiful pieces when their own ambitions were directed to making profit and providing for their growing families.

Bankruptcy proceedings were suspended in May, 1876. Before the end of the year, the factory was exhibiting in Szeged. The effects of the crisis can be judged from the comments: "The famous factory of Herend provided a modest exhibit. The financial misfortunes of this factory are well known, but they have not diminished the artistic value of its products. Yet, whereas at the Vienna exhibition the Herend exhibits dominated the Hungarian pavilion, it now shares the limelight with the products of other factories."[94]

In 1876, a very tired Fischer, still unyielding in his artistic standards, relinquished his financial burdens, handed over the factory to his sons and retired to Tata.[95] There, in his family home, he built a small workshop where, at the age of seventy-six, he could continue the creative work that had always been at the core of his life.

Thus, the golden age of Herend came to an end. It had been a period of recurrent financial crises, great success at the world fairs and a continuous striving for modernization. With their dedication and their inspired talent, the managers and workers of Herend earned the manufactory a special place in the hierarchy of European porcelain industry. In creating unique works of art without desiring to satisfy the commercial demands of a mass market, Herend continues to be recognized for its fine quality porcelain throughout the world.

ECONOMIC CRISIS
AND REORGANIZATION

1876–1920

The new management, headed by Fischer's son Sámuel, took over the factory in the firm belief that their father's preoccupation with artistic standards was the cause of the financial losses necessitating so many loans. They therefore introduced the use of transfers and discontinued the production of hand-painted porcelain. Their aim was to produce more at a lower cost, and so increase profit.

The results of this policy were not reassuring. The Fischer brothers had to acknowledge the wisdom of their excentric father and before very long they too were taking out loans and asking for substantial government aid. They were facing strong competition from the Bohemian porcelain industry—well-established, subsidized by government and based on low cost production. Again and again the brothers had to revert to the manufacturing of old products, and when they felt the need to strengthen their reputation, they depended on exhibits of old products. In the year-book of the 1879 National Industrial Exhibition at Székesfehérvár, we find the following list of exhibits: Mór Farkasházy Fischer, Tata—porcelain items, Sámuel Farkasházy Fischer, purveyor to His Majesty the King, porcelain manufacturer, Herend, Vilmos Farkasházy Fischer, porcelain-painter, Kolozsvár. As purveyor to the Court, a title inherited from his father, and with his father's products, Sámuel won a gold medal.[96] "His sons are imitating his products in Tata, Herend and Kolozsvár, but they have abandoned his artistic heritage... Their reproductions will never approach my grandfather's creations," wrote Jenő Farkasházy.[97]

In official circles there was a degree of commiseration for Mór Fischer and they invited him to join the Exhibition committee. The committee members were listed on a commemorative plaque made of porcelain, now in the Museum of Székesfehérvár. It was the last time Fischer offered his services. He died in Tata in February 1880. It was again on the strength of past glory that Sámuel gained for the factory another gold medal in 1883 at the Amsterdam Exhibition. In spite of all their efforts the Fischer brothers had to recognize failure and after eight years they sold the factory to the government. The sale was preceded by lengthy negotiations with the object of securing a post as managing director for Sámuel and a post as technical consultant for Géza. But the sale marked the end of the long connection between the factory and the name of Fischer. The brothers moved to Tata, took over their father's workshop, and operated it as the "Sons of Mór Fischer". They were never able to abandon the shapes and designs of Herend.

It was with the intention of preserving and fostering the heritage of craftsmanship and artistic skill peculiar to Herend that the government acquired the factory in 1884. This they did with the help and support of Count Pál Széchenyi and Secretary of State Matlekovics. Within a year they had sold it to a new company entitled the Herend Porcelain Factory Limited (Herendi Porcelángyár RT) with benefit of a 12-year tax exemption and a substantial interest-free loan. The painter József Eckert was appointed temporary general manager.

The new company was formed with a board of directors comprising Count Jenő Zichy, Count Géza Batthyány, Dr. Sándor Matlekovics, Tivadar Hüttl, and Mór Wahrmann. They raised the opening capital of 150,000 Austrian forints by issuing 150 bearer-shares of 1,000 Austrian forints each.

A new manager was appointed, a Bohemian, Ferenc Hippmann. He had little knowledge of the industry, nor was organization his strong point. Factory records tell us that forty-two older, experienced workers stayed with the new management.[98] Hippmann instituted piece rates so that sometimes the men took three days to paint one plate. This kind of ineffective management was repeated everywhere in the factory. In July 1888 the Independent Veszprém Gazette *(Veszprémi Független Hírlap)* reflected the public disgust when it commented: "it is not altogether inconceivable that the Bohemian manufacturer is paying his coutrymen to help ruin the world-famous Herend factory". It was an idea shared by others who saw that there was a real threat of another bankruptcy. Another Bohemian Gruss was appointed on a temporary basis until at last János Őrley was appointed Managing Director in 1885.

Modern equipment was immediately installed in the dilapidated factory buildings. Within a year large new buildings were being constructed. More rooms were added above what had been a single-story courtyard wing. A new kiln was installed with a cooling space. Skilled Sudeten-German workers were brought in from the vicinity of Karlsbad. The directors were confident that even with further investments, profit for the year could be raised to 500–600,000 forints. They were of course counting on the contribution to be made by the forty-two experienced Herend workers, and the use of all the Herend plaster moulds and designs. They were also counting heavily on the foreign trade contacts which they had also inherited and which, according to the archives, provided markets in England, France, Russia and the United States. Each individual order was recorded so that we find in the archives references such as "ordered by the German Emperor, the King of Italy, the King of Rumania..." and so on.[99]

There was no sound basis for such expansion which was undertaken in the hope of profiting from the name of Herend, and without a realistic assessment of the economic situation and the market. The workforce was increased to about eighty, but the men were badly paid, their output low, and the ratio of substandard products high. The result of all this was that year after year the factory accounts showed a loss. Bankruptcy now seemed unavoidable.

The Bohemian manager therefore abandoned the famous Herend designs and began to manufacture cheap goods, made from Bohemian raw material. In the days of Őrley, they manufactured stoneware, a policy approved by the press. "In the field of ceramics we have a splendid national heritage. It would be a noble task to use it as a basis for further developments, a task worthy of the factory of Herend." This view, expressed in the newspaper *Művészeti Ipar* could possibly have been applicable to other ceramics and porcelain factories in Hungary, but it was certainly not applicable to Herend. It was based on the unwarranted assumption that the Herend technicians would be able to devise some advanced manufacturing process for the production of new forms and designs. But Herend could not compete with the Bohemian factories, where there was a ready supply of raw material, an advanced technology and, especially for their simple yet attractive porcelain, a ready market. As for the possibility of manufacturing stoneware at Herend, such a project would have had to face strong competition from the small but established stoneware manufacturers elsewhere in Hungary. Goods from the Zsolnay factory at Pécs were popular both at home and abroad, while the name of Herend was no longer in the news. In the official report of the 1885 national exhibition there is a reference to a loss of artistic direction at Herend: "High production costs prevent Herend from competing with the Bohemians. Herend should study Meissen's 'Zwiebel Dessin' and endeavour to create a similarly marketable type of tableware heavily decorated in the tradition of Holics."[100]

These were troubled times for Herend. On July 15, 1892 they suffered a catastrophe that might well have been fatal. The west wing of the block housing the wheelers' workshop collapsed. Fortunately this occurred at the end of the working day. The last workman to leave the building witnessed the collapse. He had only just reached the courtyard when the upper floor came down with a terrible rumble, and buried all the machinery, the finished goods and the invaluable plaster moulds. The investigation headed by Őrley concluded that the cause of the cave-in was an extremely heavy load of quartz-rock stored in the attic. The report did not name anyone as responsible for the accident. Work in this part of the factory had to be suspended for a considerable period, thus adding to the financial losses already suffered.

At this point the directors decided to cut their losses. They sold out to "United Hungarian Glass-Manufacturers Limited" for 125,000 forints.[101] But this influx of capital was not very effective. The management was amateurish, unable to concentrate their resources on saleable products. However, they continued to produce

54

13

stoneware and sold an impressive number of their "Carnation" tableware products in the eastern markets.

It was now twenty years since Herend porcelain had been acclaimed at the exhibition in Vienna. Since then profits and reputation alike had been steadily declining. The secret of Herend's earlier success lay in the fact that Fischer had always been able to gauge the taste of the times and adapt his products to meet contemporary demand. When it was fashionable to admire the very early designs, he manufactured his own versions of them. He was able to meet the public need with products that were commercially successful and, moreover, *more* commercially succesful than his rivals'. By the middle of the nineteenth century, Herend not only supported itself—albeit with the aid of loans—but was a leader in the field. Fischer knew where the money was and adapted his products to please a wealthy market—the landed gentry who knew the worth of oriental porcelain.

By the end of the last century, the porcelain industry seemed to be grinding to a halt. Traditional porcelain was losing favour and the renewal of the industry now depended on the taste and needs of the middle classes who were growing yearly more prosperous. They had no wish to own imitations that were true to the point of deception. They demanded attractive but simple shapes at reasonable prices. Strong competition from stoneware factories producing tableware that was both pretty and cheap, forced the porcelain factories to change the style of their own products.

Such a transformation of production methods and production aims required great flexibility on the part of management and workforce. This flexibility was lacking at Herend. The new management was slow to recognize the contemporary taste, unprepared for change and slow to search out new markets. Certainly there was a continuing demand for Herend's beautiful old designs but the market for these beautiful pieces was fast shrinking. There is a limit to making profit out of the past. In the competitive climate of the late nineteenth century it was essential to follow new trends.

Towards the end of the century there was a movement to revitalize the national heritage in the field of applied design. It was felt that there had been too great a dependence on foreign trends. The Society of Applied Arts therefore set out to encourage modern developments of a truly Hungarian style. Their watchword was: "Let it be seen that our art originates here, that it is characteristically Hungarian, just as Viennese art clearly originates in Austria and English art in England." But to the public these ideas were no more than another passing fancy and were greeted with suspicion in the industry except at the Zsolnay factory in Pécs where traditional designs had always been used. At Herend there was an attempt to apply the new standards. New designs based on motifs from Hungarian embroidery were applied to tableware by the transfer method. The scarlet and cobalt-blue flowers were appreciated by the Minister of Commerce and proved to be a success with the public.

However, this success was not enough to halt the gradual decline of the factory. There had been too many changes in ownership, too many conflicting trends of haphazard management.[102] Under the management of Venier, brought in from Klösterle (from 1894 to 1895), the factory went bankrupt and for a brief period the doors remained closed.

It was to be a difficult task to find anyone willing to take over a factory with a history of repeated failure, especially when the aim would be to restore the factory to its former glory at a time of imponderable economic and artistic change.

The government offered to sell the factory to a younger member of the family, Jenő Farkasházy Fischer who had been living abroad—in London, Paris and Brussels. He was the son of Dezső Fischer and grandson of Mór Fischer. He was interested in the artistic aspects of the ceramics industry and had published several well-received articles on the subject. In 1893 he had accepted an appointment as art director of the porcelain factory of Ungvár. Minister of Commerce Ernő Dániel entered into negotiations with him for the sale of the factory at Herend. In this way a member of the third generation of the Fischer family came to own a company worth 80,000 forints, for which he paid only 5,000 forints while assuming the outstanding mort-gages left from various government loans.

After taking over the factory, Farkasházy (who was using as his family name the title bestowed upon his grandfather) spent some time studying porcelain factories abroad. On his return he wrote: "From all that I have learnt abroad and from what I have already observed at Herend, I firmly believe that the revitalization and future prosperity of Herend is dependent on a recognition of the factory as an institution of applied art." He underscored this statement by declaring that, apart from the Bakony beechwoods, there is nothing in the vicinity of Herend to justify the operation of an ordinary pottery. Herend's art constitutes its contribution to the industry. He repeated the necessity to renovate the buildings, overhaul the equipment and, as only one of the four kilns was suitable for firing porcelain, convert the faience kilns to porcelain kilns. The valuable models were also in need of repair.

To meet the expense of these projects and to ensure the future of the enterprise, he asked that the burden of one and one-half per cent interest on a loan of 80,000 forints be removed. For further modifications he asked for a subsidy of 10,000 forints in four equal, semi-annual increments.

He brought up the need for apprentice training schemes, pointing out that at Sèvres there was great emphasis on the education of apprentices, scholarships worth 800–1,200 francs a year being offered to five-year students.

"At present the most I can do is to fulfil the individual orders," wrote Fischer. "A stock of porcelain goods worth 200,000 forints from Herend and Ungvár are being sold at a price far below their manufacturing cost. It is therefore clear that it will be a long time before I can put my new Herend products on the market. Only the next world exhibition in Paris would provide an early hope of showing the world what I am doing at Herend and thus—hopefully—restore the fame of the factory."[103]

Jenő Farkasházy Fischer, undoubtedly a talented and skilled ceramist, started out with definite artistic ideas. These were based on his studies abroad, especially in France, as well as the experience he had gained in the factory at Ungvár. His particular interests may be deduced from his published works: *The Life and Work of Palissy* and *The Della Robbia Family*.

He started again where his gradfather had left off, with the ambition to create a new Herend style based on old Chinese and Japanese porcelain and the early designs of Meissen, Vienna and Sèvres. He manufactured porcelain in the early Herend tradition, but he also used the early pieces as a basis for new adaptations. His products were no less beautiful than those of his grandfather. He was receptive to the trends apparent, especially in France, around the turn of the century, introducing his own versions and employing the latest technology. He prepared a few individual pieces for exhibition abroad, ready to follow again Mór Fischer's formula for success. He studied and he travelled in search of knowledge. Though he had the ability to succeed as a business-man he never allowed the daily routine of the factory to prevent him from concentrating first and foremost on the artistic possibilities inherent in the porcelain industry. He was an artist as well as an industrialist and the exhibits he offered to the World Exhibition in Paris in 1900 were genuine masterpieces. The new Herend pieces were acclaimed by the wealthy aristocrats and Farkasházy received many orders.

The exhibition closed, Fischer returned to Herend, but the orders were never delivered. Elated by his success in Paris, Fischer locked himself in the factory museum, dreaming of future masterpieces, neglecting the mounting financial problems of the factory. The difficulty of combining artistic standards with profit-making was a popular theme in the contemporary press. The concensus was that on the whole it was right that the Herend Porcelain Factory should be primarily dedicated to art. Production costs were necessarily high when the raw material had to be brought from a distance and there was always the hope that some new product would be popular enough to bring in more money.[104]

It was not until 1890–1900 that a new style emerged in Europe. Munich was the birthplace of the *Jugendstil* (Art Nouveau), but it was very soon adopted in most European countries. It represented a new form of expression based on the use of flowing naturalistic flower and vegetable motifs and was widely used in interior decoration. But each nation added an individual note to the general style and when it reached Hungary it was similarly assimilated and transformed.

The spirit of nationalism engendered during the celebration of the millennium was fostered at every turn, in art as in science.[105] The new trend, with its possibilities of enrichment leading to a new Hungarian style, was everywhere made welcome. In an article in *Magyar Ipar*, Géza Márkus encouraged the people to adopt Art Nouveau: "New styles have always been associated with national or revolutionary movements. Now, in Hungary, where we have never had a strongly developed characteristic art of our own, we have the opportunity to absorb this new trend, to add to it our Hungarian heritage, and so create an Art Nouveau that is uniquely Hungarian." It was in this spirit that Hungarian artists adopted the new style—although later their efforts deteriorated into an empty formalism.

Tired of repeating past successes the painters in the ceramics industry welcomed the possibilities inherent in Art Nouveau—the forms not unrelated to the Rococo, and a new freedom in the use of colour. Some of the more exaggerated forms and designs were not well-suited to the decoration of porcelain. Plant motifs and scenes from nature were applied over the entire surface, some objects being totally overlaid with aquatic plants. Orchids and poppies were the most popular flowers, their long stems arranged in lines and braided together. A new taste in design developed, based on Japanese prototypes.

By the turn of the century Jenő Farkasházy, who made himself personally responsible for the art work in the factory, was committed to Art Nouveau. The large trays made at this time reflect a highly developed painting technique. While he basically followed the trend for deep colours and complicated designs, he to some extent achieved a more moderate effect. On some dishes the virtuosity of the painters almost lured them into painting pictures, rather than decorating porcelain.

It was due to the artistic taste of Jenő Farkasházy and his talented painters that Herend achieved a suitably restrained version of Art Nouveau. Elsewhere in the industry it was not unusual to find trays decorated with a scarlet tree-frog with lilac-coloured eyes, or an ashtray boasting a nymph with vermilion body and blue hair.[106]

Some of the most interesting developments in the art of porcelain manufacture occurred in Copenhagen, where around the turn of the century there was a progressive upsurge in the fields of art and science as well as industry. In the royal porcelain factory of Copenhagen, Arnold Krog was the first to use under-glaze painting. This was quickly adopted in porcelain factories at Bing and Grvedahl, and by Röstrand's factory in Stockholm where relief decoration on vases was also introduced. In this type of decoration he used flower motifs, especially violets, snowdrops and clover.[107]

It was not long before the Copenhagen influence reached first Meissen and Sèvres, then Berlin and Nymphenburg.

Herend too adopted these techniques, producing some original vases with the attractive "Pâte sur pâte" ornamentation. This low relief decoration was very well-suited

14

to the material, creating a subtle design in which the outline was scarcely defined. Herend also increased its production of plaquettes, so far made by only one other factory, Sèvres. Around 1900 Herend followed Zsolnay in the use of dark-glaze on simple vases. The results of these experiments were shown to the public at exhibitions in Paris, St. Petersburg and St. Louis.

According to *Art et Décoration,* the ceramics-section of the Paris Exhibition illustrated every recent development in the porcelain industry:[108] "Whereas we used to see work reflecting the talent of a few individual craftsmen we now see a multitude of styles reflecting a much higher general standard of achievement. This exemplifies the democratization of art. Today porcelain-making borrows freshly from nature, and not from second-hand sources such as books, or old documents."

At this exhibition, the Danish and French exhibits were most highly commended, with special reference to the harmonious colouring and superb technology. The simple, gentle shapes and finely shaded colouring of the Danish porcelain caused a considerable stir. The decorative effect was generally cool, northern and discreet, achieved by the use of simple flower motifs or naturalistic scenes. Earlier styles—Empire, Louis Philippe, Louis XV and Louis XVI, with miniatures, portraits and landscapes—were still in evidence, but the judges looked to the future and prizes went to the fresh innovative contemporary styles.

The Hungarian potteries and porcelain factories were well-prepared for the exhibition. They had the greatest number of exhibits apart from Japan and Germany.[109] *L'Illustration* commented that "the Hungarian contribution was almost as impressive as in 1896. Their porcelain is a worthy tribute to their long struggle for self-expression and the years of peace so recently achieved."[110] The new forms, and the vases with relief decoration exhibited by Herend were much appreciated by the experts. There was a laudatory notice in *Art et Décoration* too: "The Hungarian porcelain factory of Herend, which is one of the oldest porcelain factories … has combined perfect technology with a new floral design which is both naturalistic and colourful."

In *L'Art Nouveau* there was praise for the way in which Hungarians had emancipated their applied art from foreign, especially Viennese, influences. There was a particular reference to Herend and Zsolnay factory at Pécs.[111] The jury awarded Herend the gold medal.

The St. Petersburg World Exhibition of 1901 brought fame not only to Herend, but to the entire Hungarian ceramics industry. Of all the manufacturers of the Austro-Hungarian monarchy, only three Hungarian factories received awards: Herend, the Zsolnay factory at Pécs, and the stoneware factory at Apátfalva.[112] Herend exhibited a very small selection of pieces in the earlier styles, for in *Magyar Ipar* there had been a warning note that only works produced in the spirit of modern art would be acceptable for exhibition, the Russian people having long since ceased to admire the imitation of historical styles.

The Hungarian exhibits were therefore chosen to demonstrate the uniquely Hungarian version of Art Nouveau. Herend also received a gold medal *"pour la sculpture artistique sur vases en masse colorée"*. Farkasházy received on behalf of the Hungarian exhibitors the Medal of the Order of Saint Stanislas, third class, when he donated 90 roubles' worth of the porcelain exhibits for the benefit of poor and sick Russian children.[113]

George Vogt, managing director of the porcelain factory at Sèvres, was commissioned by the French government to visit all the European ceramics factories in receipt of awards at the world exhibition in Paris. He travelled to Herend, where he stayed for two days. Before leaving Budapest he wrote a warm and appreciative letter to his Hungarian colleagues. This was not merely a letter of thanks; Vogt, a man whose ability was recognized throughout Europe, took the trouble to pass on some of his knowledge and experience.[114] He clearly perceived the situation at Herend, recognized the difficulties, and suggested a remedy.[115]

In 1904 there was another exhibition of the latest pieces from Herend, this time at the world exhibition in St. Louis. The Herend exhibits received the rapturous approval of the Americans and were honoured with a gold medal.[116]

The Hungarian press was also kind to Herend's new style. In reviews of the Exhibition of Applied Arts which opened just before Christmas 1903, there was much praise for the wide range of distinctive colours and for the *grand feu*-glazed vases of Herend. "Some are museum pieces... They can stand comparison with any piece from Denmark, France and Saxony." The jury awarded the National Medal for the Applied Arts to Jenő Farkasházy Fischer to whom it was presented by the Minister of Commerce: "For the artistic application of fine glazes on porcelain vessels".[117]

Such recognition might give the impression that Herend had regained its former reputation. Certainly, Farkasházy was concerned to restore the reputation of the factory, and he had enough talent and organizing ability to produce some superb pieces. He did not spare himself, especially in his efforts to exhibit the Herend products in exhibitions abroad where a succession of gold medals were a token of international regard.

Unfortunately he was more of an artist than an organizer. He did not care to spend his time in supervising the factory routine. Versatile, eccentric, but easy-going, he spent his days happily in Budapest, Vienna and Paris, while the workshop deteriorated. In spite of a substantial government subsidy and a twelve-year, interest-free loan, the factory was losing money and Farkasházy was forced to apply yet another loan, and he raised 40,000 forints from the sale of machinery.[118]

Herend was the first factory in Transdanubia to establish an apprentice-training scheme, effective from July 1, 1897, with an additional government subsidy of 4,000 forints per year.[119] It was a splendid idea, but there were disappointments in practice. The initial number of apprentices was minimal, as were their wages: 50 fillérs per week. The very low rate for labourers of 8 forints per week was exceptional in

Hungary at that time when a similarly skilled worker received 25–30 forints per week in a porcelain factory abroad. This accounts for the shrinking workforce, reduced to twenty by the turn of the century and to 10–12 shortly afterwards.

Low pay also accounted for the emigration from Herend of skilled workers. Four hundred and forty-four persons moved to the United States between 1898 and 1912 from the Herend area. The factory contributed to the local rate of emigration.[120–121]

To support the population of the village it would have been necessary to employ 100–150 people. With a greatly reduced staff, limited production of commissioned work—acquired as a result of exhibitions—sufficed only for Farkasházy to make a very adequate living for himself. He did not extend his activites to provide a living for the village community,[122] and for this failure he was rightly criticized. The newspaper *Veszprémi Népakarat* had this to say: "When the government has provided a subsidy of 8,000 forints a year, a 12-year suspension of taxes, and other allowances, it has a duty to ensure that the owner of the factory fulfils his obligations."[123] Indeed, the idea of establishing a new Hungarian porcelain factory was also raised.[124]

Herend was also affected in 1907 by a general crisis in the porcelain industry. The early years of the twentieth century were notable for technological progress, yet there were no developments applicable to the porcelain industry. The Danish exhibits at the world exhibition in Paris had inspired most European porcelain factories—with the exception of Sèvres—to emulate Copenhagen by adopting under-glaze decoration in pale harmonious colours. The only major innovations were Meissen's contemporary-style "bisquits" and Nymphenburg's Wackerle-figurines—reminiscent of Bastelli's old-Nymphenburg porcelains, delicately coloured pieces which captured the very essence of the art of porcelain. There was some notable work in the Biedermeyer style, also some adaptations of naive motifs reflecting the contemporary taste for simplicity of form and design. These, however, were isolated instances.[125]

The stagnation of the porcelain industry at this time was not due to a lack of porcelain technicians, nor was it due to a lack of artistic talent. The cause was strictly economic. Foreign markets for porcelain had collapsed. Porcelain exports to the United States in 1902 were valued at over 3 million dollars from Germany, 1.5 million from France and about 1 million dollars from the Austro–Hungarian monarchy.[126] The European factories had to reduce their personnel and seek new, though less profitable, markets elsewhere. The porcelain factory of Limoges in France had to dismiss 200 workers in 1907.[127] In a word, there was in the porcelain industry a crisis of over-production, with the inevitable corollary of price-reduction and a lowering of quality. Financial uncertainties are not conducive to creative enterprise. There was no money available for either scientific or artistic experiment.[128] The markets for Herend products, at home and abroad, were greatly affected by the general economic crisis. The Hungarian market was flooded with inexpensive porcelain from Germany and Bohemia.[129] In 1908, porcelain and stoneware was imported to the value of 148,000

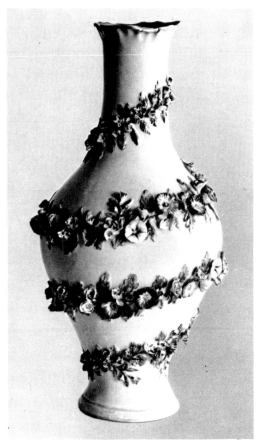

15

16

crowns.[130] Just before Christmas in 1907 the National League of Industry had appealed to the country to buy only Hungarian-made porcelain.[131] In 1907 the factory was again encouraged by an award at the National Exhibition in Pécs, and the temporary economic recovery in 1910.[132] In 1911, at the Torino Exhibition, Herend was awarded yet another gold medal.

These honours brought no decisive change in the fortunes of the factory. There were continuing financial troubles, exacerbated by the illness of Farkasházy, who now had to spend a considerable period of time in a sanatorium.

During the anxious years before the outbreak of the First World War, the situation at Herend deteriorated as the cost of raw materials and transport increased. Nor could this increased cost of production be covered by raising the price of porcelain. Wages also increased somewhat in line with the higher cost of living.

Years of economic crisis were followed in 1914 by the outbreak of the First World War. There was no demand for new dinner services or even individual pieces. Nor did the market improve, for by 1915 the price of porcelain had increased by 15%.[133] By 1916 it was a remarkable event in the village if smoke could be seen rising from the factory chimneys. The only available work was for a few painters who were completing some of the unfinished pieces stored in the warehouse. This was the state of affairs throughout the Hungarian porcelain and stoneware industries.

In 1919 the Herend Porcelain Factory gathered together some of its earlier products for an exhibition in Zurich—a last valiant gesture, since between 1916 and January 15, 1920 there was no firing whatsoever at Herend.[134]

BETWEEN THE TWO WORLD WARS

1920–1945

In 1920, when raw materials were once again available, the factory reopened with a nominal workforce.

In the post-war years of economic uncertainties, every factory had to make a fresh start. Even well-equipped and prosperous factories felt the need for enterprise. A luxury-oriented porcelain industry could not look for a market among the unemployed, nor among poorly paid civil servants. The ageing Jenő Farkasházy was quite unable to face the reality of the situation.

There was no abatement in the difficulties associated with both financial backing and the supply of raw materials, so that the factory was obliged to close down from time to time for varying periods.

Once again, the continued existence of the factory was at stake. Official circles shared Jenő Farkasházy's concern to find a way of modernizing production by introducing new technology.

Encouraged by friends, Farkasházy transformed the factory into a limited company, with the participation of the bands of Lloyd and Mobil, and with an opening capital of 500 million crowns.[135] A few shares were offered to the public, but Farkasházy retained a 50% holding, and as artistic director-in-chief, continued to manage the factory.[136]

Substantial sums were now available to the company, either for acquisitions or as working capital, but it was to be a long time before the projected modernization of the factory was completed. From time to time the company still had to ask private individuals for loans against promissory notes.[137]

Despite the difficulties, there was some progress. Within two years a housing estate had been completed, with the result that skilled workers were now attracted to Herend. A factory for the manufacturing of chamotte tile stoves was also set up, and in 1925 the school for apprentices, long since abandoned, was reopened with an intake of 44 apprentice painters and wheelers.

These were costly undertakings as may be seen from the accounts for 1925 when capital expenditure amounted to 81,000 gold crowns. The introduction of superior technology was followed by a growth in exports, primarily to France, the Netherlands, Belgium and Switzerland. During this interim period the directors had also counted on an improvement in the domestic market, but from the autumn of 1923 a period of rapid inflation threatened the whole economic structure of the nation. The public could afford to buy very limited quantities of artistic porcelain, so that the income from this source fell short of expectations.

The directors were also affected by the slump and were therefore not in a position to lend money to increase working capital. Other sources of credit had to be found. There was no hope of securing a loan from the bands; the only remaining alternative was to get loans at exorbitant interests. The future of the factory was at stake, so there was no choice. In 1925, the total debt, including interest, was 500 million crowns. Although ever since the formation of the company, production had increased yearly and production costs had always been covered—mainly by foreign sales—the repayment of interest was a growing burden which seemed impossible to diminish. The short-term loans constituted a constant threat to the very survival of the factory. Concentrating on the artistic aspects of production, and creating new designs, Farkasházy remained unperturbed by these troubles. In 1926, the year of his death, there was one last tribute to his life-work when the factory was awarded a gold medal at an international exhibition in Philadelphia.

After Farkasházy's death, the number of shareholders was increased. Men who had distinguished themselves in public life, the applied arts or industry were asked to sit on the board, among them Elek Petrovich, director of the National Museum of Fine Arts, and Dr. Jenő Hubay, director of the National Academy of Music.

The company's next task was to find a new director for the art department—a recurring problem for years to come. They also had to acquire more working capital as their debt to the Industrial Mortgage Institution was still unpaid in 1933. The company's liabilities were 138,643 pengős at the end of 1926, and 220,311 pengős on August 31, 1931.

The factory was still not as well-equipped as the better known European factories. Also, the range of products was not always in line with economic realities. The Herend reputation rested on the beautiful early designs rather than expertise in the manufacture of porcelain. Beautiful old-style table services and unique individual pieces were given preferences over the production of white porcelain. A flawless piece of decorated porcelain, whether a cup or a vase, could always find a buyer. By comparison the profit from a piece of white porcelain was negligible. Fine pieces of Herend would always maintain their value. However, in the years of the slump following World War I, there were basic changes in the home market for porcelain. In a depressed economy there was little demand for expensive good quality porcelain. Prices were too high for the majority who were concerned to afford basic needs. This was the main cause of the crisis in the applied arts industry in Hungary. This was why production at Herend was geared to the manufacture of fine early designs always in demand abroad.

Unfortunately, due to its outdated technology, Herend produced a large number of sub-standard pieces. The management expected the technical errors to be corrected by a relative of the Farkasházys, István György, a young chemical engineer with no previous experience in the porcelain industry. He was, of course, unable to cope with the problems and complaints about the quality of the porcelain were not infrequent. The directors were so concerned that in 1930 they considered closing down the factory, in spite of the fact that during the previous year they had borrowed 34,000 dollars from the Industrial Mortgage Institution. Their problems were finally resolved in a court of law where lengthy suit was fought out between István György and the directors of the company. The settlement left Dr. Gyula Gulden with 55.5% of the shares of the Herend Porcelain Factory. This made possible for him to organize the factory according to his own ideas as managing director.[138]

These important changes at the Herend factory took place against the background of the Great Depression which affected, in varying degrees, every industry throughout the world.

17

In the early thirties, in every phase of production, improvements were initiated at Herend. New machinery was installed and more systematic methods introduced. A new circular kiln was built and the stacking of the old ones reorganized to use space to better advantage, filling them with small inexpensive products and thus reducing the high cost of firing. Electricity was used for polishing, and eventually a laboratory was built. Transfer painting entirely superseded hand-painting. A favourable agreement with the Hartmuth-company permitted further developments in the production of stoves. Administrative work was accomplished by fewer employees allowing a small increase in technical staff. There was a successful drive to secure more contracts abroad.[139]

With such an efficient system of production it was now possible to concentrate on technological improvements. In 1929 Ede Telcs was appointed as art director and Emil Fischer as a technological consultant. One successful undertaking was the production of small sculptures, a useful diversification for which there had always been some need. The sculpture series, started in the mid-twenties, marked not only a new period in the history of Herend but in the history of Hungarian porcelain sculpture as a whole. Some of the subjects were not well-suited to the material, but many beautiful pieces were created. Among the early pieces we find Zsigmond Kisfaludi-Strobl's "Hussar with Sabre", János Pásztor's peasant-style "Farewell", Jenő Bory's "Hungarian Nobleman", and Éva Vastagh's small, naturalistic animal figurines characterized by fine detail, simplicity and tenderness. The influence of Ede Telcs's direction can also be seen in the later small sculptures created at Herend. He insisted always on clear outlines and an impression of strength, combined with meticulous observation.

The new company continued production of the old traditional designs but at the same time they were manufacturing less expensive services with a simple decoration to satisfy the domestic market. Simplification of traditional patterns was permitted only in moderation to avoid any danger of lowering the standard of work. Dr. Gulden described this new trend at the annual board meeting of 1933: "To achieve our aim, we are adopting methods successfully employed at the old Vienna factory, which survived the depression following the Napoleonic wars by introducing charming, artistic, but simple and therefore inexpensive designs." Around this time Malagola Cappi, an Italian practitioner of the applied arts, was attracting attention in Budapest with his very interesting lamp-shades. The factory supplied the artist with vases for which he then designed shades. It was a novel idea. In the early thirties the factory began to produce majolica souvenirs decorated in a manner reminiscent of the earthenware made at Hódmezővásárhely. It was a profitable venture but did nothing to enhance the reputation of Herend.

These experiments were not undertaken at the expense of the traditional wares which continued in production in their customary, ornate style, as we can see from the list of exhibits shown at the 1935 exhibition in Riga. By 1934 production was suitably diversified and there were healthy signs of artistic innovation. Meanwhile the factory was working on a much sounder financial basis. Sales totalled 300,000 pengős, the amount suggested by Vilmos Rosenthal as necessary to ensure viability. Progress was reflected in the growth of the number of workers. The 15–20 workers employed before the formation of the limited company had increased to 140 by 1934.[140] The artistic standard may be judged by the reception accorded to the Herend exhibits at the world exhibition in Chicago in 1933. Reviewing the exhibition Dr. József Vizsolyi commented: "I must give special consideration to the Porcelain Factory of Herend, whose products can best be described as sensational. Their impressive exhibits will long be remembered."

The thirties marked an era of triumph for Herend. The factory had survived the difficult years of the previous decade and the punishing competition of Czech porcelain manufacturers. Herend had survived when other factories had been obliged to close their doors, when even the state-owned porcelain factory of Sèvres owed its survival to a yearly subsidy of 600,000 francs.

From the mid-thirties, Herend's new prosperity was evident in every sphere of activity in the factory. After visiting Herend in 1931, Vilmos Rosenthal declared that with 160–170 thousand pengős of net yearly trade, and with sales of 300 thousand pengős, the factory could make a profit. Herend reached this platform in 1935 when borrowing was no longer necessary. Technological improvements enabled the factory to lower prices and so increase sales to the domestic market.

There was much emphasis on the artistic standard of the products in the hope of securing more foreign trade. About one-third of the factory's products were exported, but in 1934 sales to most European countries dropped significantly and it became necessary to find other outlets. Favourable publicity for Herend exhibits at an exhibition in Chicago opened up an American market. This was further strengthened by American reluctance to patronize German industry. It was now that the firm Hall House began to buy from Herend, thus initiating a relationship that has lasted until today. At exhibitions held all over the world Herend porcelain continued to attract attention. The traditional products and the Hungarian genre figurines were always popular. The "Victoria", "Sang Noir" and "Miramare" dinner services, the ornamental pieces with Hungarian motifs, and even the brown tea services previously imported from England, were all produced in ever greater numbers. Herend was again awarded a gold medal in Brussels in 1935, and a Grand Prix in Paris in 1937. The Herend entry at Riga in 1935 was much praised, also in 1936 at the exhibition in Tallin which resulted in a valuable order from the President of Estonia.[141] At the table setting competition held in Warsaw in 1936, the Museum of Applied Arts used Herend porcelain for their table, and secured for Hungary the world championship. At the Leipzig Fair, in 1937, where there were 450 exhibitors, Herend was again in the limelight, and the factory received a great many orders. There was particular praise for the Hungarian figurines, the newly created "Delphin" series, and the tableware made in the traditional style.

The Leipzig Fair convinced the trade that in contemporary interior decoration there was a place for both ornamental porcelain and figurines.

At home, the factory was once again attracting foreign, and sometimes eminent, visitors. The Prince of Wales toured the permanent exhibition housed within the compound of the factory, and admired the designs provided for his great-grand-mother, Queen Victoria, and his grandfather, King Edward VII. The Prince said that he too was an ardent collector and he placed orders for ashtrays and cigarette boxes in the "Fish" design. He was then presented with a "Prince of Wales" tea service. Franz Joseph had given the first service made in this design to King Edward VII when he was still Prince of Wales.

In the following year, at an "Old Budapest" ball in London, Herend porcelain was exhibited in a Hungarian-style pavilion where British ladies dressed in Hungarian costumes acted as sales assistants. Their first customer was the Lord Mayor of London. The fair was so successful that the display was transferred in its entirety to a large London store.

The King of Belgium purchased the "Pheasant"-design service so popular in Hun-

18

19

gary. Meantime, at the 1935 international exhibition held in Budapest, the national press did not fail to praise Herend as an important national institution.

Provincial warehouses and sales outlets were essential for success in the domestic market, hence the establishment of the wholesale house of Lavel. In another profitable venture the Herend factory collaborated with the neighbouring Glass-making factory at Ajka to produce coordinated designs for porcelain and glass tableware and even table linen. This type of cooperation between the factories continues to this day.

In the years between the wars, Herend greatly increased its production of figurines. The progenitors of all European porcelain figurines were the creations of Johann Joachim Kaendler who worked at Meissen. He was the first to recognize the sculptural possibilities of porcelain and that the use of paint on white porcelain was particularly effective on small figurines. He created colourful groups of procelain figures in a style reflecting everyday life. He began with representations of society ladies and gentlemen, court buffoons, famous actors and actresses, ballet dancers and opera singers. Later he represented the ordinary people—craftsmen, street-vendors, beggars, soldiers, peasants and children. All his figures were life-like, kindly and charming. He also created allegorical representations of abstract qualities such as love and virtue; and he personified the four seasons and the four quarters of the world.

Herend was as much influenced by the art of Kaendler as any other European factory. This is particularly evident in the Herend figurines dating from the nineteenth century, for instance the "Rooster of Herend" and "Water and Air". Very few of these were made, and they were discontinued altogether as Mór Fischer's era came to an end. Nor were they produced again until Sándor Kelety arrived in Herend when the new company was established in 1924. The number of small-sculpture designers subsequently rose to one hundred and fifty-four.

A wide range of figurines came into being, some of them amusing, all of them well-suited to the expressive qualities of porcelain. Some were created in the spirit of neo-Classicism, but influenced by contemporary taste. In all the figurines it is clear that the craftsmen of Herend were deeply conscious of the possibilities inherent in the porcelain itself. They were not so much sculptors as artists in procelain. Miniature sculptures demand clearly defined forms. They have to be "hard", because the glazing dulls the sharp contours. The artist cannot attempt the effects achieved in marble or bronze but must concentrate on the advantages offered by porcelain, especially the contrast between the purity of the white glaze and the harmony of the colouring. In the production of figurines the Herend management was wise enough to concentrate on artistic merit even at the expense of profit. It was their aim to build up a store of models both large and small, representing the finest creations of the most gifted Hungarian sculptors. Subjects chosen were many and varied, including birds, animals, oriental-style themes and human figures of peasants, priests, sportsmen, character-types and nudes as well as busts of the famous. The collection also included translucent porcelain pictures and plaquettes.

The first series of small sculptures included Kelety's bird and animal figures, then the rooster, the pair of robins, the pair of ducks and a most realistic Alsatian dog. To these were added later Andor Hubay's "Owl", Mária Lipthay's "Green Frog" and Éva Vastagh's "Rabbits".

About 150 bird sculptures and about 200 different animal figures left the kilns of Herend in the thirties. The bird sculptures were particularly colourful and gay, one of the most interesting being Kata Gácser's "Eagle". Some of the amusing animal figures were created from direct observation, notably those of Béla Márkus, Tibor Bruck's sculptures of dogs and the animal figures of Kata Gácser, András Sinkó, István Lőrincz, György Vastagh, Éva B. Lőte and Jenő Hanzély. Éva Vastagh combined humour with skill in her popular "Dog" in which she made use of the forms and colours of an old Chinese design.

Imre Huszár's "Seal" reflects his perfect familiarity with the material; his approach was modern, his style unique, and we can safely say that the "Seal" marks the opening of a new era in the history of porcelain sculpture. It proved that porcelain could be used as a medium for contemporary artistic expression: Huszár used this hard raw material to create a gently sculpted form with a surface smooth as velvet and conveying the essential character of a seal.

The peasant-type figures are mostly the work of well-known Hungarian artists, whose art is imbued with the spirit of the Hungarian countryside and a knowledge of old Hungarian folklore. A few of these pieces, no longer manufactured today, were over-decorated in a pseudo-country style which had deteriorated into mere formalism.

Elek Lux chose to immortalize a well-known figure from Hungarian folklore Ludas Matyi (Matthie the Goose Boy). He avoided the very real danger inherent in such a task of trivializing his subject to the point of banality. His "Ludas Matyi" is still one of the most popular of Herend figures, sharing this distinction with Miklós Ligeti's figurine of the actress "Déryné" (Mrs. Déry) depicted in theatrical costume.

The life of the Hungarian *puszta* is evoked for us in György Vastagh's "Csikós" (The Herdsman) and Gyula Maugsch' "Shepherd and his Dog". The "Csikós" is one of the most successful of the Herend groups; the vitality and movement in the figure of the ranger as he struggles to bridle his fiery horse in no way disturbs the closed effect of the group as a single artistic whole. As a work of art and as a technological achievement this is clearly a *virtuoso* creation.

The famous potter, Margit Kovács, a devoted student of Hungarian village life, contributed her study of a boy playing the flute. It is very characteristic of her work —imaginative, kindly, evocative of the lyric age of the minstrel story-teller. There is all the atmosphere of a fairy tale in Ede Telcs's amusing "Tom Thumb". The humour of folklore is the inspiration for István Lőrincz's sculptures which today are as popular as ever.

There were attempts to produce porcelain sculptures based on works of art in bronze, but these attempts were not always successful. Some of the porcelain figures created by Miklós Izsó and Adolf Huszár had to be re-modelled by Kata Gácser, who had a profound understanding of the technical aspects of sculptural expression. The peasant figures made on the basis of Miklós Izsó's small sketches now in the Museum of Fine Arts, the "Dancing Peasant" and the "Melancholy Shepherd", were produced in the early thirties, early examples of the art of sculpture just beginning to emerge in Hungary. Izsó created the dancing figure from observation and after many experiments. It is not intended to represent one movement but rather the spirit of the whole dance. He has achieved a fine combination of vivacity and poise. The treatment of the clothes is expressive, the folds suggesting the movement of the limbs while the decoration suggests Hungarian folk costume. In the "Melancholy Shepherd", the embodiment of national romanticism, he re-created a childhood memory. Towards the end of the 1920s, when the so-called "Hungarian baroque" was dominant in religious art, Herend started to produce religious sculptures. Although it was difficult to break away from this sentimental style, the Hungarian public was already demanding a new type in art that would express their modern life-style. Young artists

20

21

were able to break with the conservative trend, and create in a modern idiom. Elek Lux's beautiful "Matyó Madonna" is one example of this trend. The slender figure of the Madonna holding the smiling Infant is depicted in Matyó folk costume. His gift for expressing the essence and his sensitive use of the material combine to give us a pleasing work of art that has also a religious significance. At the Second Vatican Council in 1964, the Hungarian episcopate presented Pope Paul VI with several pieces of Herend porcelain, among them the "Matyó Madonna". The Pope responded by presenting to Herend the silver commemorative medal of the Ecumenical Council. There were some worthy initiatives in the design of oriental-style sculptures by Károly Csapvári, Kata Gácser, Mária Lipthay and Jenő Bory. Among the beautiful figures of nudes, traditional inspiration for artists throughout the ages, are "Woman Brushing her Hair" by Elek Lux, "Desire" by Dezső Nemes, and "Spring" by József Gondos. Éva B. Lőte's "Amazon on Horseback" emphasizes the beauty and tenderness of the female body, gently moulded in contrast to the bold contours of the powerful animal. The most popular nude figures came from the studio of Elek Lux. He always sought to express the essence of the dance and the self-contained movements of the dancer. He had no wish to develop a particular style, but rather aimed at a naturalistic representation of beauty. He interpreted the movements of the modern dancer rooted in classical forms, and this he achieved in sculptures marked by a rare strength and boldness. The "Veil-dance" is the finest of his many dancing-girl figures produced by Herend. There is a great freedom of movement in this figurine of a slender girl, depicted almost upright, arms and legs flung outwards expressing the rhythm of the dance. The movement is completed by the line of the floating veil, thus giving harmony to the whole composition. A perfect blending of form and line characterizes the "Woman Brushing her Hair". The representation of the woman's slender body and the slow movement of her arm is strictly naturalistic, something easier to achieve in this composition than in the dancing nudes, where the artist is bound by the rules of the dance.

The Herend management recognized that subjects from the world of sport would have a strong appeal for Hungarians. But the subject presents many problems for the artist who wishes to express physical effort, movement, space and the essence of a particular sport. Only an artist with a knowledge of a given sport can select a typical movement which he can re-create in a sculptural form as a work of art.

The best of these sculptures are József Gondos's "Olympic Flame" and "Hail to the Winner" reflecting the olympic spirit uniting all nations, as well as the homage due to athletic achievement. In Lajos Gády's "Skaters" we can feel the unity of momentum created in a partnership of two superb skaters. Sándor Ambrózy's "Skier" indicates the beauty of this sport through his exact representation of the movements. The artist was himself an ardent skier. A momentary pose was chosen by Lajos Barta for his "Soccer Player". Béla Pankotai Farkas's "Wrestlers" is a skilful representation of a classic movement of Graeco-Roman wrestling, for he has chosen to depict the

74

moment when one of the wrestlers lifts his opponent off the ground. It is a work as worthy of the art of sculpture as it is of the ancient sport. "Start" by Géza Fekete evokes the intense concentration of the swimmer just before he dives.

In some sculptures the reality of the sport has been lost in the effort to create a work of art. For instance the muscular figure of the "Putter" bears little relation to the characteristic movements of the player, and the rigid posture of the "Discus-thrower" misses the swinging movement of that sport.

Busts of famous personalities have come from the studios of János Horvay, István Lőrincz, Dezső Erdey and Jenő Hanzély. These sculptures are representational, created from life and were made to commemorate illustrious figures of various nationalities in the fields of music, politics, literature and the arts.

The translucent plaquettes of various sizes depict landscapes or politicians and other public personalities of the time. Joined by lead-glazing, a number of large translucent and rather rare porcelain plates fill a window of the Roman Catholic church of Herend. As the light from the outside shines through the slightly convex, unpainted porcelain plates, it brings out the plasticity of the shapes. The window was designed

DAL VATICANO, 26 Ianuarii 1966

Rev. me Domine,

Officiosae epistulae tuae respondens, numero distinctae 8600-52/
1965 atque die 10 huius mensis datae, tecum communicare propero
Augusto Pontifici perquam accepta obtigisse dona, affabre quidem con-
fecta, quae opifices ex porcellanica fabrica in urbe Herend, pietatis
causa, Ipsi miserunt.

Cum vero de muneribus, abs te allatis perdurante tertia Sessione
Concilii Oecumenici iam tibi litterae gratias agentes rescriptae sint
die 20 novembris 1964 n. 34398, te rogo, ut de iis etiam, quae tempo-
re quartae Sessionis exhibita sunt, egregiis istis viris, Beatissimi
Patris nomine, grati memorisque animi sensus significare velis.

Christi autem Vicarius dilectis istis filiis atque eorum propin-
quis prospera cuncta ex animo ominatur, atque Apostolicam Bene-
dictionem, supernarum gratiarum auspicem, dilargitur.

Interea, qua par est observantia me profiteor

Tibi addictissimum

+ I. Dell'Acqua
Sebst.

Rev. mo Domino
D. no Doct. ALEXANDRO KLEMPA
Administratori Apostolico
Veszprimiensi

by Károly Csapvári, and today the style is carried on in Herend by the young artist László Horváth.

Since the twenties when small sculptures were first manufactured at Herend, there has developed a tradition for preserving the best of the early models while constantly initiating work on new themes.

In 1939 Hungary was not immediately plunged into the Second World War, and although the economy was depressed by manifestations of German aggression, production figures at Herend for 1939–40 show no trace of these uneasy years. Indeed, the figures showed a steady improvement throughout the thirties. In 1937, the kiln-capacity grew by 86.3%, wages rose by 8–10%, and the factory produced some 15,000 items per month. The number of employees in 1923, when the company was founded, had been 32, but it reached 450 in the years of 1939 and 1940. Production rose by 10% above the level of previous years. Of the total production 18–20% was sold abroad, but exports to England and the United States were reduced by 25% in 1938.[142]

Before the Second World War, in 1937, Herend again exhibited at the world exhibition in Paris and again received an award. Herend's traditional products and some of the small Herend sculptures were the focus of attention. In 1938 in Berlin, Herend received a Letter of Distinction at the International Handicraft Exhibition. In 1939, the gigantic New York World Exhibition brought both honours and financial success. Herend established an extensive American representation, which is still active today. In 1940, at the 7th Triannual of Milan, Herend was awarded a "Diplome d'Onore". The Hungarian factory was now in the forefront of the developments which for two decades had characterized the European porcelain industry.

In 1939 and 1940, in spite of the mounting difficulty of securing raw materials, the factory continued production. This was primarily due to an unexpected rebound in the domestic market caused in its turn by the increased purchasing power of those now finding employment, also by the hoarding instincts of those who in wartime were seeking valuable objects as an investment. In the early forties, as the economic effects of the European war spread across the world, Herend had to face new problems —restrictions on ocean-going cargo transport, the freezing of traditional sources of raw materials and the loss of skilled workmen to the armed forces.

The management concentrated on maintaining standards and satisfying the demand for new designs. It was Dr. Gyula Gulden who devised a scheme to improve the factory's balance sheet during the war years. After studying the market very carefully at home and abroad, in 1943 he founded a separate company, using his own capital, the Handicraft Merchandising Company, which acted as a sales agency for Herend. He bought consignments of merchandise from the Herend factory, receiving a 10% commission for selling it to his chosen outlets. He was also appointed as Consul in

Portugal during the war years, and with the help of the neutral Portugal, he was able to ensure sales abroad. Portugal had already in 1938 purchased goods from Herend valued at about 1,500 pengős, but Portuguese orders between 1940 and the end of 1943 were valued at 55,514 pengős. In this way, the factory continued to operate through the years of war.

The accounts for those years show that the production of stove tiles increased substantially in 1940. This was the result of the iron shortage which prevented the production of iron stoves. In 1941 the cost of paste, glaze and paint amounted to 73,636.13 pengős, and the total profit for that year was 2 million 195 thousand pengős. More machinery was ordered from the Ganz factory and in 1943 a new stove-tile kiln was installed. This capital expenditure permitted a 50% increase in stove-tile production (already amounting to 40,383 pieces). Export trade was valued at 134,804 pengős in 1938, while in 1943 the figure rose to 425,302 pengős. We should point out that in 1943 the war-time economy was already leading to concealed inflation and currency devaluation so that the 1943 growth was not proportionate to increased production. This is substantiated by the fact that the Minister of Public Supply in 1943 authorized Herend to raise prices by 90% instead of 18% as in previous years. During the war years the factory lost its export markets in England and France, and from 1942, in the United States. Export markets still open to Herend were Germany—with whom there was a two-way trade—Switzerland, Portugal, Slovakia, Italy and Belgium.

It is clear from the factory records that permission to manufacture ornamental porcelain for export was given only on condition that the factory would produce technical and military porcelain components. These goods were indeed made at the factory, but only as an experiment. They were not produced in quantity, merely as a token of military commitment to satisfy official circles. The factory was accordingly listed as a supplier to the armed forces and the workers made subject to military regulations.

In 1944, as fuel acquisition became difficult, the working hours were reduced, and the number of employees dropped, as many were drafted or forced to work at the harvest. The number of 750 employees in the early war years was reduced to 630 in 1944, and even these were mostly apprentices and women. Also, the number of firings had to be reduced sharply. At this time, the factory began to manufacture ornamental-tile ovens modelled after originals.

Since the late 1930s, Herend followed certain artistic trends. In specializing each stage of production it became possible to perfect the production process, while at the same time raising the artistic level of the porcelain. The production of porcelain sculptures was reduced from 20% to 5%. Until 1938 figures had always been hand-painted; now colours were blended with the paste thereby retaining the essential contribution of the porcelain material as well as the primacy of the figure. Ágoston Brand originated this process. Experiments were also conducted by Imre Somorjai to discover a similar

78

23

way of decorating ornamental pieces and tableware. Some products resulting from his experiments are "Vase with Swallows", the "Service with Apple Blossom", and a number of ornamental trays. All are now in the factory museum.

Everyday needs were also catered to. These products were produced to a high standard, the tastes and buying power of the ordinary people being considered as carefully as those of the privileged few. The less expensive merchandise was widely advertised in contemporary trade magazines. These well-made and attractive products satisfied both domestic and foreign markets and created a firm financial basis for the factory where new products were constantly being tried out.

During the forties, Herend employed eight artists on a permanent contractual basis. The sums expended on artistic projects in 1942 exceeded the yearly profit average of the twenties.[143]

Throughout the troubled 1940s, the Herend factory continued to use the finest raw materials, to apply elegant decorations, and to retain the old forms and designs while searching continuously for possible innovations. The management could always adapt to new circumstances as when, faced with wartime taxes on the use of gold leaf, they introduced attractive coloured borders on tableware and made use of a lustre finish. The reputation of Herend was preserved.

There were other innovations. Heraldic designs were used on various ornamental pieces, and naturalistic, vividly coloured bouquets were designed for the most delicate porcelain. István Lőrincz's tea service, Piroska E. Richter's dinner service for children, and Géza G. Fekete's figure of a woman carrying a jug are all pioneering creations in a new style that yet upholds the Herend tradition.

In 1938, István Lőrincz, a sculptor who had worked in the factory for many years, committed himself to porcelain, and devoted himself to the creation of models for production at Herend. He became director of the art department, in which capacity he played a very active part in the life of the factory. His aim as an artist was to discover a sculptural style most suited to the creation of small porcelain sculptures. He began to make neo-baroque figurines, some of them remarkably successful, for instance "Suzanna" and the "Fontana". He would undoubtedly have perfected the technique had it not been for the ever-growing frustrations of the war years.

Other works by a new group of enthusiastic and hard-working artists include Lívia Papini Kuzmik's "Adam and Eve", Éva B. Lőte's "Amazon", Dezső Erdey's superb "Széchenyi" bust, Elek Lux's "Bathing Woman", "Corpus" by Ernő Jálics, "Saint Steven on Horseback" by Ferenc Sidló, Jenő Hanzély's "Matyó Harvest" and "Fawn of the Pasture". The "Geisha" by Károly Csapvári recalls in theme and design the Herend style of the nineteenth century.

These pieces were first exhibited to the public in 1942 at the First National Hungarian Ceramics Exhibition, where the products of the Herend Factory received lavish praise. The factory received a letter of distinction from the minister for culture and István Lőrincz was awarded the Gold Medal of Budapest.

Tibor Bruck's 13-piece "Hunter" service was also exhibited there, along with Eta Holéczy's tea and coffee services.

Tibor Bruck's "Hunter" design was based on his own observation of the Hungarian sports of hunting and shooting. He elaborated this idea for other table appointments moulded in the form of plants or decorated with forest motifs—a salt-sprinkler in the shape of a mushroom, small groups of mushrooms used for card-trays, coasters decorated with painted animal heads, tureen handles in the shape and colour of a spray of oak leaves and acorns, of knobs like strawberries or hazelnuts. The early nineteen-forties saw the creation of a number of individual pieces bearing the Herend trade-mark, together with the "Pin-Herend" mark and the signature of the artist. In the catalogue of the 1943 Hungarian National Exhibition of Applied Arts in Kassa (now Košice) there are appreciative references to the creations of Sándor Ambrózy, Kata Gácser, Imre Huszár, István Lőrincz, Éva B. Lőte, Elek Lux and György Vastagh. This spirit of determined creativity denies the truth of the saying so often repeated in wartime: "Inter arma silent Musae" (The Muses fall silent in battle).

AFTER THE LIBERATION OF HUNGARY
in 1945

The war left the Herend factory buildings intact, but the economic and artistic basis of the enterprise had to be rebuilt. It was one of the first factories in Transdanubia to re-open its doors. When production started again there were 180 workers and 3 kilns.

For the next three years there was a struggle for survival.[144] The most serious task was to secure an adequate supply of essential raw materials. It was estimated that the factory could operate for one year at about 40% capacity using up the materials left from the pre-liberation days.[145] In this difficult situation the management had to be flexible. They decided to manufacture articles requiring only small quantities of the precious "white matter", even though it meant more work. The directors favoured elaborate design requiring longer hours of work in the art department. This increased need for the painters' skill ensured the future of one of the factory's most valuable traditions.[146] At the same time the alarming decrease in the number of wheel-operators employed was a threat to production.

In the hope of attaining some degree of stability, the factory was trying to find more up-to-date methods of marketing. After so many years of turmoil there was little demand for porcelain at home. It was therefore essential to produce goods attractive to foreign buyers. The mechanics of the trade demanded shipment of goods which were paid for at a later, sometimes a much later, date. This entailed loss of interest on working capital, but until 1948 no alternative arrangement was available. At the same time lack of demand in the domestic market resulted in stock-piling at the factory. This in turn necessitated cutting the production. Yet overheads remained as before.

Herend was heading toward financial disaster. A paste-substitute was introduced and production time reduced to forty hours per week.[147] The situation in 1946 and 1947 is reflected in desperate appeals to the National Planning Board: "Shortage of paste now threatens our very existence... We are doing everything possible to secure sufficient quantities of raw material to keep 400 workers occupied... We have no raw material at all..."

The urgency of this petition is a measure of the relief felt at all levels of the factory when it was included in the nationalization programme on March 2, 1948. The records provide evidence of government assistance and factory progress after 1948.[148] The fifties were marked by unprecedented capital investment, acquisition and modernization. New installations included wheel and paint shops, kilns, 12 new electric kilns for the decorative work, electric dryers, running water and central heating, the adaptation of existing kilns for butane or propane heating, the building of separate art studios and a two-storey office building. For the benefit of all employees the management provided a clubhouse, sport-fields, a new factory museum and, above all, the training school which had so often been tried and abandoned in the past, usually because of lack of interest on the part of the authorities. New buildings comprising a school and a hostel were erected. There the apprentices were taught, by the latest methods, the basics of aesthetics and the technology and skills of the porcelain industry.[149]

The housing conditions of the workers were also improved. The small, roughly constructed peasant homes once so typical of the Herend region disappeared, and were replaced by blocks of spacious apartments equipped with all modern conveniences.

Basically, the technology of porcelain-making in Herend has not changed. Shaping and painting are still done by hand, and it is precisely this individual, hand-made effect that puts Herend porcelain in a class of its own. Now machines knead and clean the paste, most of the wheels are power-driven and the old wood-burning kilns have been replaced by electric kilns. Most of the delivery work has also been modernized. The quality of all the raw material is tested in a well-equipped laboratory. Here too the finished goods are checked and new experiments constantly initiated with a view to perfecting the composition of paste and glazes.

As the market expanded, production had to be increased. The kilns were therefore enlarged and the flow of production speeded up with no lowering of the standard of work. From a technical and artistic point of view Herend products were now well known and new export markets were found in Australia, the Bahamas, Yugoslavia, Mexico and the Soviet Union.

As our culture was in the process of change, Herend, too, was modernizing its views of art. In search of new forms, this trend was a direct consequence of the great changes that affected architecture. The concept of space became an integral part of architectural design, and this, in turn, had affected other fields of art, including the art of porcelain, which, in retrospect, encompassed a total aesthetic concept.

Any consideration of the significance of porcelain in a changing society will elicit a number of varying opinions. The love of porcelain is seen by some as the token of a snobbish adherence to a past era when it was made only for privileged members of the ruling classes. One could protest that it should be cherished for its own unique qualities, the purity of the white, its delicacy and translucence. It might be valued

24

because of its hygienic characteristics or because it can contribute to a pleasing contemporary environment.

The applied arts have always had a notable place in Hungarian history; the Herend Porcelain Factory, for example, has helped preserve the heritage and to maintain national tradition, while enriching it with a unique contemporary contribution of its own. This contribution, especially the most delicate Herend tableware, has been acclaimed throughout the world.

The value of Herend tableware is undoubtedly augmented by its hand-painted decoration, whose designs are always made to suit the form of the object. Another factor in Herend's excellence is the talent and imagination of its artists. As far as small statuettes are concerned, they have changed to suit the decor of today's modern interiors.

The problems facing Herend today are not with its tableware, but mostly with its small porcelain figurines. What may have been interesting in architecture had an adverse influence in this area of sculpture, where the geometric, simplified forms and the stressed functionalism of the porcelain objects contributed to a disruption in the development of small sculptures in Europe after World War I. This uncertainty was reflected in a prolonged period of eclecticism, which characterized not only Herend, but also the other European factories. In search of a new style, they favoured the neo-rococo sculptures at this time, and Herend, too, joined the trend in the late thirties.

In creating sculptures the malleability of the paste is extremely important, enabling the artist to handle it sensitively. Porcelain-paste is eminently suitable for this task and will always be in demand for this reason. The sculptor creates a work of aesthetic appeal far removed from the elaborate, gilded designs so much admired in the past. He uses his material to give outward form to an aesthetic ideal, which is nevertheless dependent on the basic qualities of his chosen material. But the personality of the artist equally determines the final product; it is he who finds new ways of expressing the essence of a work of art. Artists in Herend today can make use of a long tradition in their art, but are, nevertheless, forced to always produce something new. This is the basis for Herend's continued success: the creation of unique, innovative products based on refined artistic tradition.

In the applied arts there can be no rigid demarcation of styles. One style may easily merge into another. At Herend, artists are encouraged to experiment; the only trend to have been actively discouraged was the move toward rootless non-figurative abstract forms produced by a fashionable, international élite. Respect for tradition must necessarily limit the scope for innovation in the designs for Herend tableware. But the small figurines now being produced at Herend have a quality of their own which transcends temporary innovation and will always appeal to the sensitive eye and the responsive heart.

This lyric quality can be found in, for instance, "The Nursing Deer" by Sándor Farkas of Boldogfa, and in "Girl Playing the Harp" by Jenő Hanzély. These are but two of the gifted artists who now devote their talents to the preservation of the Herend tradition while at the same time responding to all that is best in contemporary trends, all that can be incorporated in that tradition and so strengthen their heritage for future generations.

Four names stand out in the area of design of tableware and ornamental objects: Ágoston Brand, Éva Szittya Horváth, Irén Cs. Illés and Emese Vásárhelyi. Éva Szittya Horváth is imaginative in her creation of original forms and in her use of colour and glaze. In the last few years she has produced a number of vases and ornamental pieces which display her talent to the full. Her tableware is characterized by a search for an economy of expression, and the designs are enriched by harmonious colours, as in her Empire-style "Josephine" service. The range of her interests and her creativity are reflected in her persistent experiments in the production and application of glazes.

A wide knowledge of the history of art has enabled Éva Szittya Horváth and Ágoston Brand to create services in the manner of styles from earlier periods—Empire, Renaissance and Biedermeier. The Renaissance service was the biggest challenge, as there was in that era no porcelain in Europe and therefore no model. They had to study the Renaissance interior, acquire a feel for it and create a characteristic form for each

84

25

separate piece. They studied the design of very small Renaissance ornaments now in museums and then, by fusing all their individual discoveries, created a design reflecting the glorious age of King Matthias Corvinus; hence the name of the service, "Beatrix".

The achievement has been to transmute for the delicate medium of porcelain the designs created for an age of splendour. The festive appearance of the service is emphasized by the gold ornamentation on a cobalt-blue background.

The "Duna" service of Éva Szittya Horváth and Ágoston Brand is influenced by the late Biedermeier style and relates very well to the simpler versions of that type of furniture. Unlike the early Biedermeier pieces, the handles of the tureen and cups are shaped as organic parts of the whole. The relief decoration in purple and gold is unostentatious and is typical of Biedermeier craftsmanship.

Irén Cs. Illés created both small and large services in the contemporary European idiom. The forms are always well-balanced, the design an attractive combination of the new and the traditional. The clean lines of her pieces are in the Herend tradition. She applies elements of Hungarian folk-motifs very successfully, and always after much research to ensure a nice blending of form and decoration. Her "Bakony" coffee service is an exceptionally beautiful example of her style: the motif of the Hungarian shepherd wearing a long felt cloak brings a sense of the past to a service designed for modern life. The gilded relief scattered in haphazard fashion over a background of bright red and blue, creates an effect that is as charming as it is original.

Emese Vásárhelyi knows how to continue the Herend tradition as seen by her coffee service with its fine filigree work. Her service earned Herend acclaim at exhibitions home as well as abroad, as for example the Premio Internacional España in Valencia. Two artists now creating small sculptures for Herend are Jenő Hanzély and János Tóth. Hanzély has been active for many years at Herend as may be seen from the variety of his work. His early sculptures are naturalistic, but he has since experimented with new ways of expression. There is a movement in his sculptures which not only serves to create a sense of space but also expresses a spiritual quality and makes each creation at one with its surroundings. His new works are profoundly lyrical, the decoration very restrained. They reflect his own joy in beauty and in life itself. He disdains all tricks, leaving his figures to make their own impact. One of his most beautiful sculptures is the "Girl-Rider", a lyric creation of unusual nobility, with

26

sensitive and simple outlines, perfectly balanced in the finest traditions of sculpture. Hanzély enjoys a nation-wide reputation as an artist whose creativity seems to be renewed in each successive work. He has profound knowledge of the history of sculpture as may be seen from his more recent works in which he interprets and transmutes the sculptural achievements of past eras in various parts of the world. The movements of his figures are detached from any specific period in time, and they are imbued with the contemporary spirit. This is well demonstrated in his "Geisha Girls". The sculpture reflects the characteristics of porcelain and of the period, and it is also a unique interpretation of figures in space. In the decoration and virtuoso painting he preserves the traditions of Herend.

For the Austrian city of Stockerau, he created in Herend a bust of Nikolaus Lenau over 1 metre in height. The white porcelain bust stands on a green pedestal of polished granite and blends harmoniously with the surrounding buildings. The porcelain seems to reflect the personality of this son of two neighbouring nations and the lyricism of his poems more intimately than either bronze or stone.[150]

János Tóth's sculptures are the product of much reflection, determination and hard work. They reveal his deep respect for the porcelain itself, while conveying emotion through simplicity of form. He faithfully follows his own realistic and individual style. He selects his themes from nature—studies of birds, fish, and wild animals. In his most recent works, his aim is to express the essence of his subject rather than the detail.

The young artist Ákos Tamás makes his small figurines with great dedication; he is able to combine modern technology with a knowledge of traditional methods. A good example of his work is his series "The Musketeers".

The youngest artist of the factory is László Horváth, who has shown himself to be very adaptable in his attitudes and who has already demonstrated his ability by creating new tableware and by developing a transparency technique. The clean lines and gentle colours of his vases place them unerringly in line with the most beautiful old creations of Herend. His engraved tea and coffee service exemplifies the modern interpretation of the Herend tradition for which he received a gold medal in Faenza.

Herend porcelain is not always designed in the factory's department. Free-lance artists are sometimes given commissions or are invited to enter design competitions. It is still the Herend policy to manufacture porcelain designed or sculpted by the greatest of Hungarian artists. Among those who have made their contribution to the Herend tradition are Zsigmond Kisfaludi-Strobl, Pál Pátzay, Zoltán Olcsai Kiss, Imre Huszár, Barna Buza, Ágoston Brand, Tibor Bruck and Mrs. István Torma.

Zsigmond Kisfaludi-Strobl was inspired by a theme from Hungarian history when he created his sculpture "The Archer", to commemorate the 1971 World Exhibition of Hunting held in Budapest. He depicts the hunter the moment after he has shot his arrow. Horse and rider are as one, co-ordinated in their dynamic forward thrust. The factory presented the first copy to Prince Philip, husband of Queen Elizabeth of

England, and a guest of honour at the exhibition. It was a rare opportunity for Herend to acknowledge the support received from the British royal family in the early years of struggle for international trade.[151]

Zoltán Olcsai Kiss's candlestick, the "Shepherd" recalls the life of the Hungarian plain. The stylized figure of the shepherd is accentuated by the faint outlines of folk motifs on his long felt cloak.

Pál Pátzay has created a new interpretation of the traditional theme, the "Horseman". The sheer honesty of his approach is particularly endearing.

Barna Buza feels a strong commitment to the Herend tradition to which he adds a contemporary quality in the harmonious lines of his "Polo player". His "Domestic

27

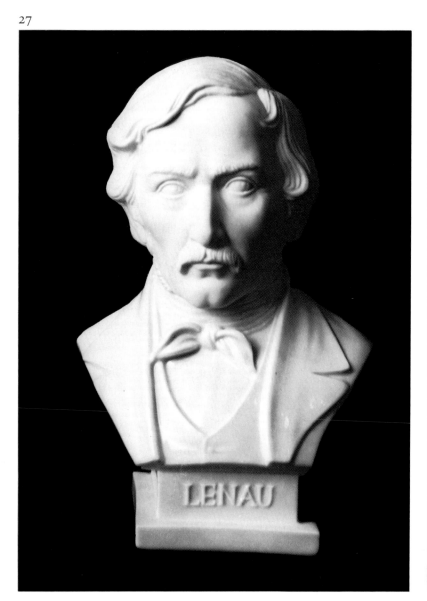

28

Altar" is an innovative representation of a religious theme. His portrayal of Christ and the Madonna in anguish is free of pathos and yet full of dramatic tension. The discreet pastel colouring and the decoration create a liturgical atmosphere and enhance the plasticity of the work. The decoration was designed by Tibor Bruck, and reflects his lively imagination. Tibor Bruck is very closely associated with Herend. His services owe their charm to his gift of drawing and his talent for design, as for example his "Pompadour" service, "Hunter" service and the one bearing his fruit design.

The artistic aspects of the porcelain industry are in flux. The general public is often insufficiently informed of the experimental attitudes of the artists who create the tableware. The artist is happy if his creations are understood and liked. Both artist and public want to see a beautiful product that serves a genuine need.

The Herend policy is to allow nothing to come between the factory and the public. The retail sales outlets may be a practical necessity but Herend has never fostered its own isolation. On the contrary, the Herend museum has served to forge an important link between those who make the porcelain and those who appreciate it, buy it and use it. Since its inception there has been a constant increase in the yearly number of visitors. In the November 28, 1939 issue of the newspaper *Magyarország* (Hungary), the average yearly attendance was given as between ten and twelve thousand. Last year more than one hundred thousand people visited the museum.

New designs, new products and the latest techniques are displayed at all the great world exhibitions, also at the International Fair in Budapest, the Industrial Exhibition held in Szeged, on various exhibitions of porcelain in other countries, and at the National Travelling Exhibition. Criticism and praise stimulate the creation of new designs. Innovations do not necessarily follow in the wake of public opinion, but there is always a realistic appraisal of views expressed and these serve to guide future activities. Such was the case after the very successful, independent exhibition of Herend products held in Paris during April, 1970. Herend was anxious to learn whether their production policy was approved by foreign experts. Paris and the French art critics were able to see not only the best work of Hungarian artists but also the versatility of Hungarian applied art. The porcelain was displayed in separate interiors arranged in the style of different periods and was much praised in Paris and elsewhere in Europe.

Similar success awaited Herend at the exhibition held in Vienna in the spring of 1973 to commemorate the Vienna World Exhibition of 1873. The exhibits were chosen to demonstrate the one hundred years of development and progress.[152]

The history of the Herend Porcelain Factory shows clearly that the name of Herend does not merely signify one of Hungary's numerous industrial enterprises. It is a name linked with that of Meissen and Sèvres, and the three are factories unique in the history of porcelain manufacture, famous for their forms, their designs, their painted decorations. Herend takes its place with them, while it retains Hungarian tradition.

The progress of the factory demonstrates that the pursuit of artistic standards and excellence of quality is rewarded by a success that can never be achieved where commercial aims are paramount.

The fame of Herend does not rest on the talent of a few individuals but on the concerted efforts of the entire factory and the favourable response of the public.

Visitors to the factory sense the spirit of Herend which is still alive today. They are greeted warmly in each department where it is noticeable that a great tradition is in the hands of a younger generation. These young people are fully conscious of their responsibility, worthy recipients of the capital investment provided to ensure the future of Herend, and worthy of Kossuth's own vision of its excellence.

29

ILLUSTRATIONS IN THE TEXT

1. Cream-jug, sugar bowl and pot (M. Fischer period, 1844). Museum of Herend.
2. Female figures (M. Fischer period, 1840). Museum of Applied Arts, Budapest.
3. Ornamental plate with a scene of the burning factory (1840). Museum of Herend.
4. Cup with relief decoration. Capo di Monte's influence (1840s). Museum of Herend.
5. Ornamental plate with chinoiserie design (1846). Property of the author.
6. Tea service and plate with "Parsley" design (1850s). Present-day application of the original design.
7. Ornamental plate with chinoiserie design (early 1850s). Museum of Herend.
8. Ornamental plate with chinoiserie design (early 1850s). Museum of Herend.
9. Ornamental plate with chinoiserie design (early 1850s). Museum of Herend.
10. Portrait in porcelain of Alexander v. Humboldt (1857). Museum of Applied Arts, Budapest.
11. Coffee service with "Balatonfüred" design (1858). Museum of Applied Arts, Budapest.
12. Vase with two handles, with the portrait of Prince Albert, husband of Queen Victoria (late 1860s). Museum of Herend.
13. Fruit bowl with figurative ornamentation (late 1870s). Museum of Herend.
14. Ornamental plate with a copy of Millet's "The Angelus" (turn of the century). Museum of Herend.
15. Coffee pot (turn of the century). Museum of Herend.
16. Vase with relief decoration (1900). Museum of Herend.
17. Ducks (Sándor Kelety, 1924). Museum of Herend.
18. Veil-dancer (Elek Lux, 1929). Museum of Herend.
19. Woman combing her hair (Elek Lux, 1929). Museum of Herend.
20. Gordon setter (György Vastagh, mid-1930s). Museum of Herend.
21. Déryné (Mrs. Déry) – (Miklós Ligeti, 1936). Museum of Herend.
22. Skaters (Lajos Gadi, 1941). Museum of Herend.
23. Geisha (Károly Csapvári, 1936). Museum of Herend.
24. The Rape of Europa (Jenő Hanzély, 1950). Museum of Herend.
25. Girl-rider (Jenő Hanzély, 1963). Museum of Herend.
26. Reclining nude (Jenő Hanzély, 1967). Museum of Herend.
27. Bust of Lenau (Jenő Hanzély, 1972). Museum of Herend.
28. Woman holding a candle (Mrs. I. Torma, 1967). Museum of Herend.
29. Horseman (Pál Pátzay, 1975). Museum of Herend.
    Inner endpaper, front: The court-yard of the factory is depicted on a copperplate by István Élesdy.
    Inner endpaper, back: Copper plate with illustration of the Herend Porcelain Factory (István Élesdy).

COLOUR PLATES

1. Ornamental jug (individual piece, M. Fischer period, 1846). Museum of Herend.
2. Ornamental dish with "Miramare" design (M. Fischer period). Museum of Herend.
3. "Bouquet de Saxe" tea service with gilded ground. Museum of Herend.
4. Coffee pot with "Kugler" handle. Painted blue, with engraved scales, scattered fruit decoration. Cup and saucer with "Bouquet unique" design (M. Fischer period). Museum of Herend.
5. Coffee service, "Kugler" shape, purple scales, "Liechtenstein" garlands. Museum of Applied Arts, Budapest.
6. Fruit bowl with gilded pedestal (M. Fischer period). Museum of Applied Arts, Budapest.
7. Ornamental vase in baroque style with a picture of the factory (M. Fischer period). Museum of Herend.
8. Dessert dish with scenes from Watteau (M. Fischer period). Museum of Applied Arts, Budapest.
9. Coffee service with "Balatonfüred" design (M. Fischer period, 1858). Museum of Herend.
10. "Gödöllő" tea service (M. Fischer period). Museum of Herend.
11. Samovar. Presented by Franz Joseph to the Russian Tzar. (Copy, M. Fischer period). Museum of Herend.
12. Coffee service with reticulated background and framed Hungarian folk-scenes (M. Fischer period, 1862). Museum of Herend.
13. Cups with chinoiserie design (design from the M. Fischer period).
14. "Empereur" coffee service (M. Fischer period, about 1860). Museum of Applied Arts, Budapest.
15. "Fleurs des Indes" dinner service (design from the M. Fischer period).
16. Ornamental plate with "Cubash" design (M. Fischer period, about 1858). Museum of Herend.
17. "Apponyi" coffee service (design from the M. Fischer period, about 1860).
18. "Sang jaune" dinner service (design from the M. Fischer period).
19. "Petites roses-d'or" smoking set (design from the M. Fischer period).
20. Plate in original "Sang Noir", chinoiserie design (M. Fischer period). Contemporary statuette in "Sang Noir". Museum of Herend.
21. Ornamental vase with chinoiserie design (M. Fischer period, about 1860). Museum of Applied Arts, Budapest.
22. Bonbonnière with "Poissons" design. And another with a view of Tihany Abbey. (Both are from the M. Fischer period). Museum of Herend, and Museum of Applied Arts, Budapest.
23. Cane and umbrella stand with "Esterházy" design (M. Fischer period). Museum of Herend.
24. Tea service (M. Fischer period). Museum of Applied Arts, Budapest.
25. Pierced fruit bowl surmounted by flower vase (M. Fischer period). Museum of Applied Arts, Budapest.
26. Tea service with "bird" motif (design from the M. Fischer period). Centre-piece with "Rothschild" design.

27. "Victoria" dinner and tea service (M. Fischer period, 1851). Museum of Herend.

28. "Miramare" tea service (design from the M. Fischer period). Museum of Herend.

29. Ornamental tray with Queen Maria Theresa and her son, the future Emperor Joseph II, receiving the oath of allegiance from the Hungarian nobility (1862). Museum of Applied Arts, Budapest.

30. Ornamental dishes with pierced rim and scenes from Watteau (1873). Museum of Applied Arts, Budapest.

31. Coffee service with "Waldstein colore" design (design from the M. Fischer period, the coloured version from the turn of the century). Ornamental basket with "Fleurs des Indes" design (design from the M. Fischer period) Museum of Herend.

32. Ornamental vase (1890). Museum of Applied Arts, Budapest.

33. Centre-piece with "Bouquet de Herend" design. Museum of Herend.

34. "Tupini" dinner service (1890). Museum of Herend.

35. Creamer with "Motifs hongrois Grand" design (1890). Museum of Applied Arts, Budapest. Contemporary table lamp and tea service with the same design.

36. Teacup and saucer (about 1890). Museum of Applied Arts, Budapest.

37. Table lamp with oak leaves (turn of the century). Museum of Herend.

38. Vase, "pâte sur pâte" technique (turn of the century, J. Fischer period). Museum of Herend.

39. Mantelpieces (turn of the century, J. Fischer period). Museum of Herend.

40. Vase with chinoiserie design (about 1880). Museum of Herend.

41. Ornamental dish with latticed rim, water-fowl design (turn of the century). Museum of Herend.

42. Decorative candlestick and ornamental vases (1880–1890). Museum of Applied Arts, Budapest.

43. Cobalt vase with goat's head handle (turn of the century, J. Fischer period). Museum of Herend.

44. Hussar with sabre (Zsigmond Kisfaludi-Stróbl, 1927). Museum of Herend.

45. Dancing peasant (Kata Gácser, after Miklós Izsó, 1938). Museum of Herend.

46. Farewell (János Pásztor, early 1930s). Museum of Herend.

47. Seal (Imre Huszár, 1939). Museum of Herend.

48. Amazon on horseback (Éva B. Lőte). Museum of Herend.

49. Olympic flame (József Gondos, 1939). Museum of Herend.

50. Matyó Madonna (Elek Lux, 1939). Museum of Herend.

51. Girl with pitcher (Géza G. Fekete, early 1930s). Museum of Herend.

52. "Duna" dinner service in Biedermeier style (Éva Sz. Horváth and Ágoston Brand, 1973). Museum of Herend.

53. Hunter and lady with dog, rococo style (Jenő Hanzély, 1966). Museum of Herend.

54. Lady reading (Jenő Hanzély, 1970). Museum of Herend.

55. Princess Elizabeth of England on her pony (Zsigmond Kisfaludi-Stróbl, 1938). In porcelain: 1969. Museum of Herend.

56. The Rape of Europa (Jenő Hanzély, 1950). Museum of Herend.

57. "Beatrix" dinner service, Renaissance style, cobalt-gilt decoration (Éva Sz. Horváth and Ágoston Brand, 1971). Museum of Herend.

58. Geishas (Jenő Hanzély, 1972). Museum of Herend.

59. "Josephine" dinner service, Empire style (Éva Sz. Horváth and Ágoston Brand, 1965). Museum of Herend.

60. "Pompadour" coffee service, rococo style, engraved and painted (Éva Sz. Horváth and Ágoston Brand, 1964). Museum of Herend.

61. "Bakony" coffee service (Irén Cs. Illés, 1972). Museum of Herend.

62. "Shepherd with his Donkey" candlesticks (Zoltán Olcsai Kiss and Éva Bakoss, 1967). Museum of Herend.

63. "Lily of the Valley" vase, "Goblet" candlestick (Irén Cs. Illés, 1973). Museum of Herend.

64. "The Archer" (Zsigmond Kisfaludi-Stróbl, 1971). Museum of Herend.

65. "Dubarry" dinner service, baroque style (Tibor Bruck, Éva Sz. Horváth and Ágoston Brand, 1964). Museum of Herend.

66. "Beatrix" coffee service, Renaissance style (Éva Sz. Horváth and Ágoston Brand, 1972). Museum of Herend.

67. "Snowdrop" breakfast set, engraved (László Horváth, 1967). Museum of Herend.

68. Nursing roe (Sándor Boldogfai Farkas, 1954). Museum of Herend.

69. Fish (János Tóth, 1966). Museum of Herend.

70. Spoon-bills (János Tóth, 1957). Museum of Herend.

71. Boy playing the flute (Margit Kovács, 1936). Museum of Herend.

72. Giraffes (Jenő Hanzély, 1960). Museum of Herend.

73. Polo player (Barna Buza, 1967). Museum of Herend.

74. Harpist (Jenő Hanzély, 1935). Museum of Herend.

75. Domestic porcelain relief altar in wrought-iron frame (Barna Buza and Tibor Bruck, 1968). Museum of Herend.

PORCELAIN MARKS

Fischer Moricz Herend 842	FISCHER MORICZ HERENDEN 42 S	HEREND 1843	F.M. 843 HEREND
Herend 844	MF HEREND 845	Herend 846	FM HEREND 846
FM HEREND 847	MF Herend	MF .3. I.	a Herendi Porzellan gyár HEREND 847
HEREND 1855 №25	N°.1. ℓHa 1855.	Herend 1862	1871
	HerendiGyár	Herend	MF

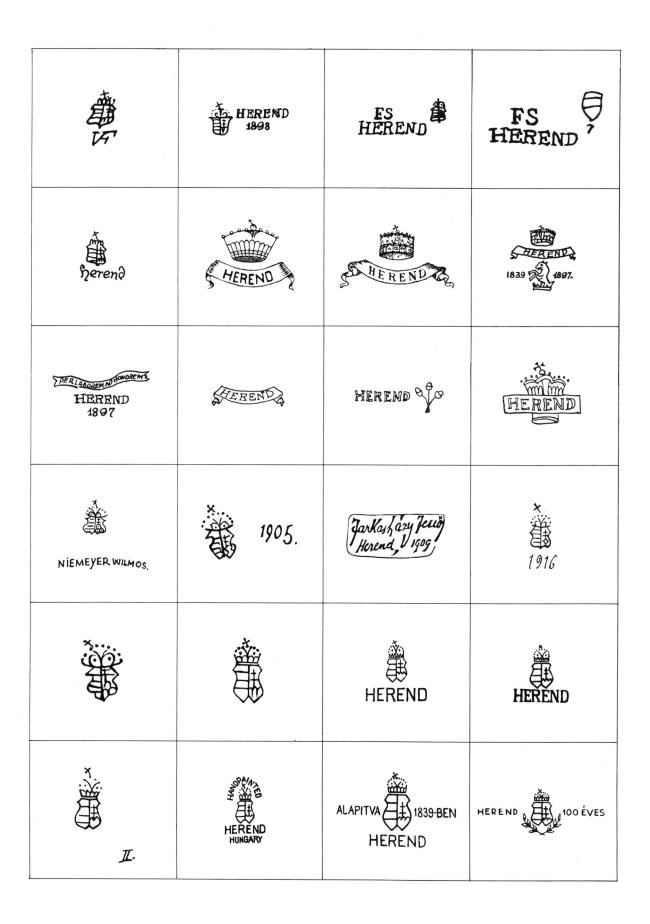

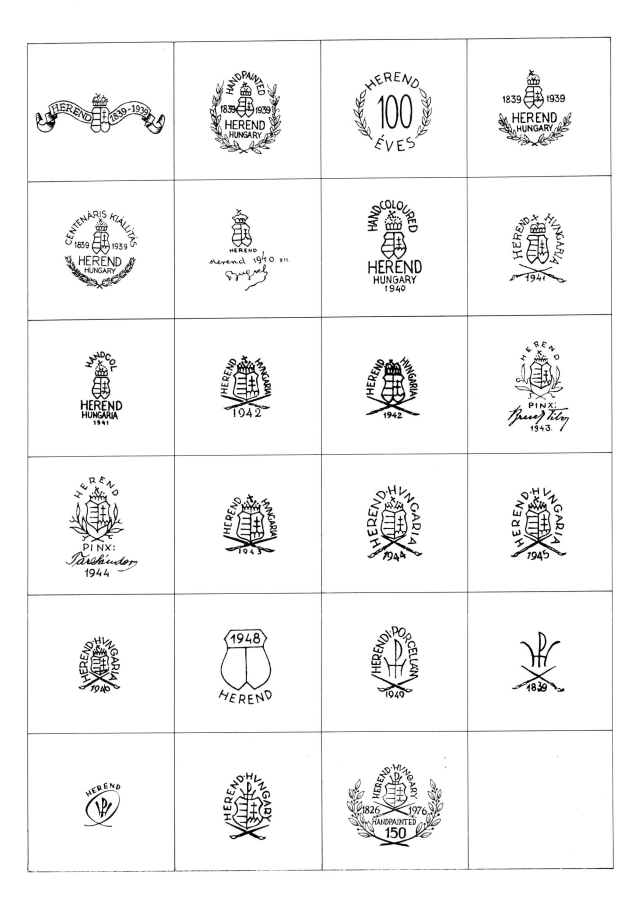

COLOUR PLATES

2

3

4

5

6

7

8

12

14

15

16

17

18

20

21

22

23

24

26

27

28

29

30

31

35

36

37

39

41

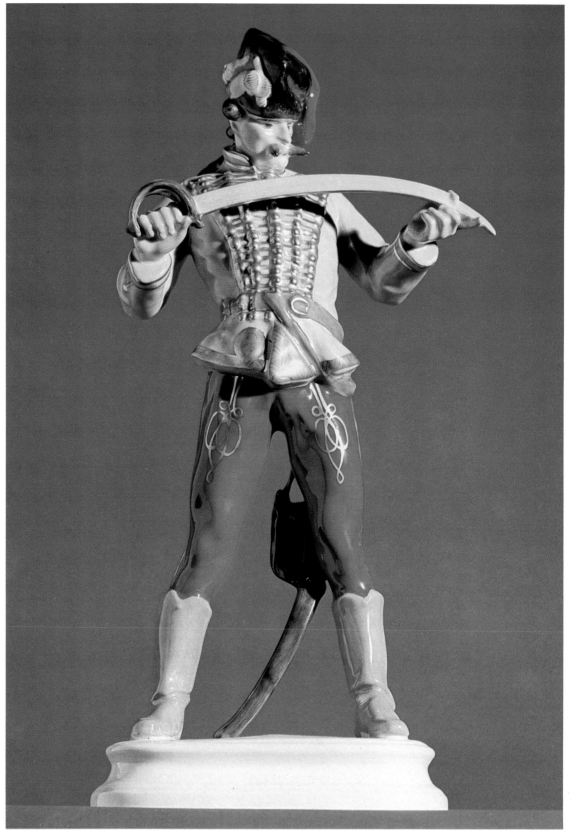

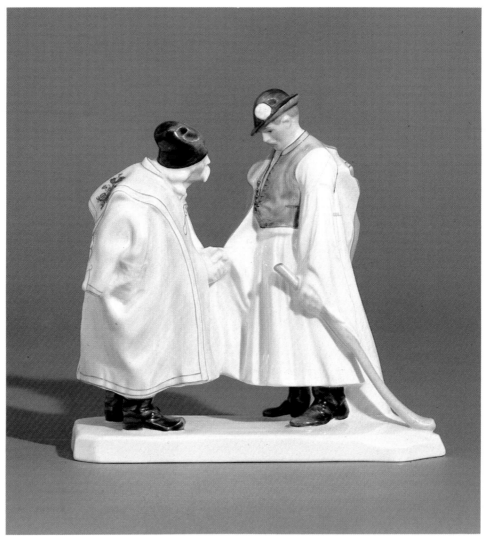

46

47

48

55

60

61

62

63

64

65

66

67

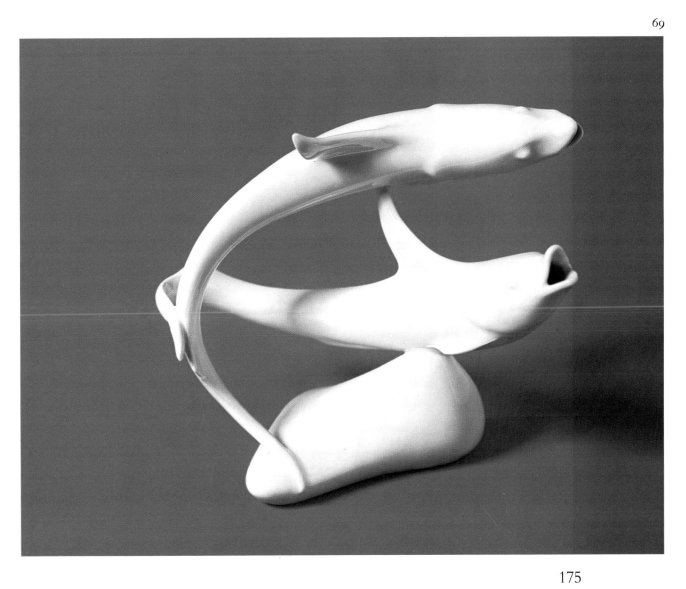

70

71

72

73

74

75

NOTES

Abbreviations in the notes:

VAL = *Veszprémi Állami Levéltár*
      (State Archives, Veszprém)
OLT = *Országos Levéltár* (National Archives)

1. From Lajos Kossuth's address at the Second Industrial Exhibition, August 21, 1843

2. Judit Koós. "Kossuth szerepe a magyar iparművészet történetében" (Kossuth's Role in the History of Hungarian Applied Arts). *The year-books of the Museum of Applied Arts.* I, 1954. Kossuth brings to the reader's attention the products of Hungarian industry, such as Herend porcelain and other outstanding Hungarian merchandise, asking craftsmen to exhibit their work to the people, bringing to light a "talent otherwise lost in obscurity".

3. Imre Holl–Pál Voit. "Hunyadi Mátyás Budavári majolikagyártó műhelye" (Matthias Hunyadi's Majolica-manufacturing Plant). *Antiquities of Budapest.* XVII, 1956

4. Béla Krisztinkovich. *Haban Pottery.* Budapest, 1962

5. Károly Csányi. *A magyar kerámia és porcelán története és jegyei* (The History and Trademarks of Hungarian Ceramics and Porcelain). Budapest, 1954

6. The high price of Chinese porcelain can be appreciated from the agreement made in the early 1700s between the King of Prussia and the reigning Prince of Saxony when the Saxon Prince received 100 dragoons from the King of Prussia for 124 pieces of Chinese porcelain.

7. Erich Köllmann. *Meissner Porzellan.* According to a report to the King on March 28, 1709, *"... den guten weissen Porcellain samt der allerfeinsten Glasur und allem zugehörigen Mahlwerk welcher dem Ostindianischen wo nicht vor, doch wenigstens gleichkommen soll".*

8. Augustus turned the factory into a veritable fortress. He guarded it with armed troops, trenches and drawbridges, and ordered the death penalty for entry without permission. Yet his secret was finally discovered by a daring enterpreneur. Du Paquier, a quarter-master in the service of the Austrian government, travelled to Meissen, where he formed a pact with two French adventurers who were lurking about the factory entertaining a similar hope of discovering the secret. Bribery was the weapon with which they arranged for the factory chemist to escape to Vienna where the Viennese porcelain was then founded.

9. Otto Walcha. *Porzellan*

10. Dezső Futó. *A magyar gyáripar története* (History of the Hungarian Manufacturing Industries). Figures illustrating the backwardness of the Hungarian manufacturing industries around 1840: in a population of 12 million there are 117,156 craftsmen and 8,413 frontier soldiers. This means that in Hungary there was one craftsman for every 78 persons. The figure for Austria is 15.

11. Sándor Mihalik. *Folia Archaeologica.* VI, 1954.; Vera Sümeghy. "A herendi porcelán" (Herend Porcelain). *Építőanyag.* 1954

12. Sándor Mihalik. *Folia Archaeologica.* VI, 1954.; "Adatok a regéczi porcelángyártás történetéhez" (Data Pertaining to the History of Porcelain Manufacturing at Regécz). *Művészettörténeti tanulmányok.* 1957

13. Earlier publications also speak of Stingl's activities: Vince Wartha. "Az agyagművesség" (Working with Clay). Decision of the Royal Hungarian Central Court in the György-suit of 1936 (P. XXII. 400.659/95): "The porcelain factory of Herend was founded by the porcelain-maker Stingl, his partner being Mór Fischer."; Dr. Béla Dornyai. "A herendi porcelán műipartelepről" (Concerning the Porcelain Manufacturing Plant at Herend). *Pesti Hírlap.* II, 1842; Dr. József Varga's expert opinion of the porcelain factory of Herend, 1934. (Archives of the factory)

14. VAL. Minutes of a meeting held on June 2, 1828

15. VAL. Minutes of a meeting, 1826. *Mestermunka*. II, 1966. "1826. The year of the founding of the porcelain factory of Herend."

16. VAL. Minutes of meetings (80/944) 1826

17. Minutes of the General Assembly, Veszprém (1613) May 20, 1833 and 1835. "Ferenc Vintsigel has constant financial problems. After borrowing various sums of money, he offered his home in Herend as collateral for 300 forints to Mátyás Winter, owner of the stoneware factory of Pápa. Vintsigel could not pay the interest, nor repay the principal. Winter instigated legal action but died without receiving his money. Later, under the burden of debt, he put his home on the market and it was bought by Stingl."

18. VAL. Court Records (K. IX. Nr. 143) 1834

19. VAL. Minutes of the General Assembly (p. 797, Nr. 637) June 2, 1828. From Domonkos Stökel, parish priest of Kislőd 1730 forints; ibid, (K. X 155) 1834. From Canon János Szmodits, 389 forints; ibid, Court Records (K. X. Nr. 143) 1834. From Canon János Küllei, 261.19 forints; ibid, minutes of the General Assembly (V. II. p. 370, Nr. 953) 1829. From Canon Sándor Kolósváry 150 forints

20. Sándor Mihalik. "A városlődi régi kerámia" (Traditional Ceramics of Városlőd). *Folia Archaeologica*. 1955

21. VAL. General Assembly (2345) 1837 János Mayer, a stoneware-making apprentice, immigrant from Jamova, Bohemia, comes to the factory of Mátyás Winter in Pápa.

22. VAL. General Assembly (35.629, 299.1073, 1572. 2902) 1840. Bertalan Kéri. "A pápai keménycserépgyár története" (The History of Pápa's Pottery). Dissertation

23. VAL. Minutes of the General Assembly, (1227, 1228, 299) 1840 (489) 1841

24. Herend Factory Archives. The estate of Jenő Farkasházy Fischer. Jenő Farkasházy Fischer's petition of 1922. "According to the documents in my possession, my grandfather spent 26,785 gold forints for the building of the factory, between 1839 and 1841."

25. *Pesti Hírlap*. February 2, 1842

26. VAL. Minutes of the General Assembly (Nr. 3) January 3, 1842. Minutes of a meeting (Nr. 125) February 7, 1842

27. The first Hungarian Industrial Exhibition was opened on August 26, 1842 in the redoute-building at Pest. Lajos Kossuth reported the event in his article entitled "Report from the first Hungarian Industrial Exhibition" as commissioned by the Board of Directors of the Chamber of Hungarian Industry. The exhibition closed on September 21, 1842. There were 213 exhibitors and the number of visitors was 14,425.

28. *Internationale Sammler Zeitung*. Wien, 1921

29. VAL. Minutes of the General Assembly, 1843–1845

30. VAL. Minutes of the General Assembly (Nr. 25) January 2, 1844

31. VAL. Minutes of the General Assembly (Nr. 1877) 1843 (Nr. 439) 1877

32. The holding company documents from the factory archives.

33. Ibid.

34. Ibid.

35. Ibid.

36. Countess Colonna. *Les Arts en Europe*. Musée des Arts Décoratifs, Paris (Br. 2708)
    VAL. Minutes of the General Assembly (Nr. 2089) 1845

37. *Hon*. (Nr. 268) 1871

38. *Gazdasági Hírlap*. XIII, 1933. The transaction between Paris and Herend in 1845

39. *Pápai Hírlap*. 1933

40. OLT, Budapest. Ministry of Agriculture, Industry and Trade, Department of Industry. Documents (6–20) 1848

41. *The Christian Science Monitor*. Boston, 1927

42. Olivér Mészáros. "A minősítő remek fejlődése" (The development of masterwork). Dissertation

43. Herend Factory Archives

44. Mór Gelléri. *Világkiállítások és fejlődése, rendszeresítése* (World exhibitions, their development and classification).

45. *Illustrierte Zeitung*. Leipzig, 1851

46. Report of the German Customs-Union, 1853 Verlag der Deckerschen Geheimen Ober-Hofdruckerei

47. *Mittheilungen über die Industrie-Ausstellung aller Völker zu London im Jahre 1851. Wien, aus der Kaiserlich-Königlichen Hof und Staatsdruckerei*. 1853

48. Municipal Authority of Prague (11,084) 1847
    VAL. Minutes of the General Assembly (Nr. 2325) 1847

49. *Magyar üveg és agyagújság* (Hungarian Glass and Clay News). 1905

50. Bericht der Pest-Ofner Handels und Gewerbekammer Im Jahre 1853

51. Two years after the first international exhibition in London, England's exports rose from 74 to 99 million pounds sterling. The organizers of the exhibition realized that all the advantages afforded by the exhibition could easily be maintained by creating a museum with a permanent exhibition open to the public. With this in view the famous South-Kensington Museum was estab-

lished in the year of the exhibition, the aim being to educate industrialists and public alike in standards of industrial and domestic design. The exhibition also resulted in the foundation of apprentice schemes.

52. The contemporary Parisian press publicized the exhibition well in advance. *Le Moniteur Universel* commented: "A Londres l'exposition était industrielle, à Paris elle sera artistique." Bibliothèque Nationale de Paris Lc–2, 113/114. *Le Moniteur Universel* (Journal officiel de l'Empire François, 1855, Exposition Universelle)

53. *Pester Lloyd.* 1855
Pest-Ofner Localblatt. 1855. "The Paris Exhibition, by a compatriot living in Paris: … I must draw attention to Mr. Fischer's porcelain made in the Herend Porcelain Factory, near Veszprém, Hungary. All Hungary's friends are extremely happy to see these magnificent pieces from a Hungarian factory. Mr. Fischer had the good judgement to place the bust sculptures of Their Majesties, the Emperor Franz Joseph and the Empress Elizabeth in the foreground where they commanded general attention."

54. Factory Archives. Cash book 1858

55. Factory Archives. World exhibition 1855. Report of the international jury, Volume II, issued under the direction of His Imperial Highness, Prince Napoleon, president of the Imperial Committee.

56. Year-book of the secondary school of Székesfehérvár. 1871/72; Dr. Béla Dornyai; "Über die Herender Porzellan-Industrienlage". *Wiener Zeitung* (Nr. 278) 1857

57. *Hon.* 1871

58. Annual Report of the Pest-Buda Chamber of Commerce and Industry. 1860–62

59. Béla Felek. "A 125 éves Herendi Porcelángyár technológiájának története" (One hundred and twenty-five years of technology at the Herend Porcelain Factory). *Építőanyag.* 1964

60. National Archives, Budapest. Documents of the Chamber of Industry. 1863

61. Géza Vásonkeő. "Ungarische Spezialitäten". *Die Donau.* September 26, 1869. The author discusses the Herend factory in detail. He was personally conducted round the factory by Mór Fischer who recounted the following anecdote: a few years previously he had received a visit from Princess Schw. who showed him a vase, given to her by a member of the British royal family, but now broken. Pointing to the companion piece of the broken vase, the Princess asked him if he could make such a superb piece for her. Fischer looked at the vase for some time, then smiling he showed the Princess his own trademark, saying: "Since I already made two of them, I believe I can manage a third."

62. Déri Museum, Debrecen. (Inventory number: DF. IV. L/279. a.) There is a blue Herend mark on the bottom of the plate with the year 1868. (Diameter: 25.2 cm)

63. Countess Colonna. *Les Arts en Europe.* Musée des Arts Décoratifs, Paris (Br. 2708)

64. J. Falke. "Fischer-féle porcellán gyártmányok az osztrák múzeumban" (Fischer porcelain products in the Austrian museum). *Wiener Abendpost.* 1864. Factory Archives, Herend

65. J. Falke. op. cit.

66. Déri Museum, Debrecen. (Archive Nr. D.F. IV. I/279. a.–b.). Both trays of the lower part of the fruit-pedestal bear the under-glaze "Herend" mark. Written in blue over the glaze, one shows the year "1861" and the initials M.F., the other shows the year "861", the initials M. F. and "No–9".

67. *Hon.* 1871. The porcelain, faience and stoneware manufacturers' trade journal published an enthusiastic detailed report on the Herend porcelain exhibited in Paris.

68. Prof. Carl Diebitsch. "Ungarisches Porzellan, Herend." *Die Schaulade.* I, 1958. "Die einfachste Nachahmung kann nicht als sklavische Nachahmung angesehen werden denn jede hat irgendeine Eigenheit und einen besonderen naiven Reiz der Herender Künstler, einstiger Bauernjungen."

69. *Luzerner Neuste Nachrichten.* Land. Bibliothek. Bern (Zf. 1032–1933 Nr. 300) 1933. "Das beste chinesische Porzellan stammt aus Ungarn."

70. Bibliothek Oestr. Museum 737. Die Industrie-Ausstellung von 1862 von Lothar Bucher, Berlin, 1863. Gerschel

71.–72. National Archives. Budapest. Documents of the Chamber of Industry. (Nr. 967. 52) 1865

73. Factory Archives. Business records. 1867

74. *Wiener Zeitung.* 1868

75. Factory Archives. The Holding Company documents. Notes of Jenő Farkasházy

76. Factory Archives. The Holding Company documents. Appraisal of the Herend porcelain factory. 1929

77. Colonna, op. cit. *Arts Décoratifs,* Paris

78. Colonna, op. cit.

79. National Archives. Royal Hungarian Ministry of Internal Affairs (Nr. 5002) December 25, 1867

80. National Archives, Budapest. Ministry a latere. General documents, Royal books (Vol. 68. p. 422. 19.2944) 1870

81. Mór Fischer's reply to the Chamber of Commerce and Industry. February 6, 1867

82. General catalogue of the national exhibition in celebration of the millennium. 1896

83. National Archives, Budapest. Ministry of Agriculture, Industry and Commerce (22957) 1869 and (24839) 1869

84. *Wiener Weltausstellungs-Zeitung.* October 29, 1873

85. Factory Archives. Reports of the judges at the World Exhibition, Vienna. 1873. France, Commission Supérieure. Reports (Vol. III. k. Paris, Imp. M.) 1875. Victor de Luynes. *Keramik und Glasware*

86. *Wiener Weltausstellungs-Zeitung.* 1873

87. *Industriezeitung für Ungarn.* 1873

88. *Internationale Sammler-Zeitung.* Wien, 1921

89. VAL. Meeting extraordinary of the General Assembly (Nr. 459/5524) July 13, 1874

90. VAL. Meeting of the General Assembly (430/3829/74)

91. Factory Archives. Inventory, 1867–1898. In the Royal Law-Court of Veszprém the company was declared bankrupt on August 4, 1874 (Order Nr. 5378/1874). An inventory dated August 31, 1874 of Herend goods at the Vienna depot was produced in court. According to the Court Order these goods were valued at 25,925.90 forints, which sum was seized for the benefit of creditors.

92. *Anyagi érdekeink* (Our financial interests). IV, 1876. "The value of both Austrian and Hungarian securities has decreased substantially in the past few weeks, by about 4–5% as to the Hungarian, and by about 1% as to the Austrian ones."

93. VAL. Office of the County-Prefect. (Nr. 3425–6495) July 30, 1874

94. *Anyagi érdekeink* (Our financial interests). 1876

95. Dr. Vincze Wartha. "Az agyagművesség" (Working with Clay). *Magyar üveg és agyagújság.* (Nr. 1/29) 1905

96. Album of the National Exhibition of Industrial Crafts, Produce and Livestock held at Székesfehérvár in 1879. Edited by dr. Adolf Szalóky

97. Factory Archives. Posthumus writings of Jenő Farkasházy

98. Factory Archives. Documents from the holding company period

99. Ibid.

100. *Művészi Ipar* (Industrial Art). 1885/86. Imre Szalay's report on industrial art at the National Exhibition

101. Purchase agreement between the Herend Porcelain Factory Limited and the United Hungarian Glass-manufacturers Limited

102. Yearly report of the Győr Chamber of Commerce and Industry. 1873. Assessment of the local economic situation

103. Factory Archives. Jenő Fischer's petition to the Minister of Commerce. February 3, 1897

104. János Pap. *Magyar Ipar* (Hungarian Industry). 1897–1938.

105. Dr. József Földváry's lecture on December 12, 1897, in the Chamber of Commerce and Industry, at Kassa

106. *Magyar üvegipar* (Hungarian Glass-industry) (Nr. 18) 1901. "Műízlés a kerámiában" (Artistic taste in ceramics)

107. *Magyar üvegipar* (Nr. 19) 1901. "Secessio az agyagiparban" (Art Nouveau in the ceramics industry)

108. *L'Illustration.* "L'art à l'Exposition". Musée des Arts Décoratifs, Paris (Nr. 2419) 1889

109. *Magyar üvegipar.* 1901

110. *L'Illustration.* "La Céramique à l'Exposition". Musée des Arts Décoratifs, Paris (Nr. 2419) 1900

111. *Magyar Iparművészet.* 1901. "L'Art Nouveau"

112. *Magyar üvegipar.* 1901. "A magyar kerámia sikere" (Hungarian success in the field of ceramics)

113. Information received from the Leningrad secretariat of the Hungarian-Soviet Association for Friendship

114. *Magyar Ipar* (Nr. 20) 1901. György Vogt, director of the Sèvres Porcelain Factory, in a letter to Jenő Farkasházy Fischer: "You, Sir, managed to guide your factory in the only direction which is to be followed from both an artistic and a technological point of view."

115. *Magyar üvegipar* (15. 8) 1901. "Elismerés a Herendi Porcelángyárnak" (Congratulations to the Herend Porcelain Factory)

116. Mór Gelléri. *Amerikai világkiállítás körül* (A tour of the American World Exhibition). Budapest, 1904. The exhibition was opened on April 30, 1904 by Theodore Roosevelt, President of the United States.

117. *Magyar Iparművészet.* 1903.

118. Ibid.

119. Factory Archives. Company Documents. 1928.

120. *Magyar üveg és agyagújság,* 1903. "A herendi porcelángyárról" (Concerning the Herend Porcelain Factory). "Instead of 100 workers, we find only 2 wheel-operators, 6 painters, 3 apprentices, 2 day-workers—13 people in all."

121. The yearly report of the Chamber of Commerce and Industry. Győr, 1903

122. The state allowed Fischer to offset some of his debts against the 3,182 crowns earned for merchandise sold

in St. Louis, and the 2, 215 crowns earned for sales in Milan. Factory Archives. Jenő Fischer's petition to the Minister of Commerce. 1910. *Magyar üveg és agyagújság*. 1903. "A herendi porcelángyárról" (Concerning the Herend Porcelain Factory)

123. *Népakarat*. 1901. (Weekly paper of Veszprém, covering the interests of shop-keepers, industrial and agricultural workers)

124. *Magyar üveg és agyagújság*. 1906

125. *Keramisches Jahrbuch*. Berlin, 1909. "Künstlerische Fortschritte in der Keramik seit 1900"

126. *Magyar üveg és agyagújság*. 1902

127. *Agyagipar*. 1907. "A porcelánipar helyzete" (The state of the porcelain industry)

128. *Keramische Jahrbuch*. 1909.

129. *Magyar üveg és agyagújság*. (1/215) 1910. "Az agyagipar jelenlegi helyzete" (The current state of the clay industry)

130. *Magyar üveg és agyagújság*. VIII, 1908

131. *Magyar üveg és agyagújság*. 1907. "The Christmas of the Hungarian industry"

132. Yearly report of the Chamber of Commerce and Industry. Budapest, 1910.

133. *Magyar üveg és agyagújság*. 1916.

134. Factory Archives. Jenő Farkasházy Fischer's petition, 1922: "In the year of 1916 I had no choice but to suspend the operation of my last kiln, when it was taken to the fields of battle." (Commerce Ministry 9473/1922)

135. Factory Archives. Agreement reached with the Banks Mobil and Lloyd on July 9, 1923. (County prefect's licence Nr. E 4724–923)

136. Factory Archives, company records. 1923. Records of the Chamber of Commerce and Industry in the Győr County Archives. The name of Jenő Farkasházy cancelled and re-registered. (Book of registration Cg. 272/1923, Nr. Cg. 82/2–1924)

137. Factory Archives, records. 1925

138. Factory Archives, company records. 1930

139. Factory Archives, company records. Minutes of the meeting of the Board of Directors. May 11, 1929

140. *Honi ipar*. 1934

141. *Pester Lloyd*. III, 1936. Factory Archives. Price-list sent to Riga

142. Győr Chamber of Commerce and Industry. 1938. Assessment of the economy

143. Factory Archives. 1944. Records of meetings of the Board of Directors

144. Factory Archives, correspondence. 1945. Report of the Herend Porcelain Factory to the Győr Chamber of Commerce and Industry. Production did not begin.

145. Ibid.

146. Progress Report of the Herend Porcelain Factory. 1947. Records of the General Assemblies. 1947

147. Report of the Herend Porcelain Factory, December 12, 1947 to the Minister of Industry

148. The Herend Porcelain Factory, minutes. April 8, 1948.

149. Progress Report. 1948. Inventory. 1948.

150. *Pannonia Magazin für Mitteleuropa*. M. 1974 II, Margit Pflagner. "Wie kam es zur Enthüllung der Lenau-Büste?"

151. *Die Schaulade*. No. 8, 1972. "Auf der Weltjagdausstellung". At the World Exhibition of Hunting in Budapest, Dr. Győző Sikota, art manager of the Herend Porcelain Factory, presented to Price Philip, husband of the Queen of England, "The Archer", a small porcelain figure by Kisfaludi-Stróbl.

152. *Cercle Diplomatique*. (2. Jahrg. 3–4) 1973. "Porzellankunst aus Herend—in Wien" (eröffnet im Collegium Hungaricum von Dr. Győző Sikota, künstlerischer Leiter der Feinkeramischen Werke in Budapest); *Burgenländisches Leben*. (Heft 4/5) 1973. Margit Pflagner. "Porzellan von Herend. Kunstgewerbe aus pannonischer Tradition."